REAL SOUPS
& SAUCES

By the same author

Microwave Cooking Times At A Glance!
The Combination Microwave Cook
Microwave Cooking Properly Explained
The Microwave Planner
Microwave Recipes For One

Uniform with this book

REAL SOUPS & SAUCES

Annette Yates

RIGHT WAY

Typeset in 10/11pt Times by Letterpart Limited, Reigate, Surrey.
Printed and bound in Great Britain by Cox & Wyman Ltd., Reading, Berkshire.

The *Right Way* series is published by Elliot Right Way Books, Brighton Road, Lower Kingswood, Tadworth, Surrey, KT20 6TD, U.K. For information about our company and the other books we publish, visit our web site at **www.right-way.co.uk**

CONTENTS

Illustrations by
Lindsay Thomas

INTRODUCTION

How often I have pondered over a simple bowl of steaming soup served alongside a wedge of cheese and a chunk of bread, or a smooth and colourful sauce spooned over a piece of steamed fish or grilled meat. There is no doubt that a home-made soup or sauce can make something fairly ordinary into something really special.

Real Soups and Sauces has provided a welcome opportunity to collect together the recipes that are most often made in my kitchen.

As usual, my family and friends have all been eager to taste the recipes and I thank them for their observations and suggestions (usually ranging from the politely couched to the bluntly honest). I have special thanks for my mother who has enjoyed making up many of the soups "just to double check they are OK". My daughters Emma and Lindsay, nephews David and Michael, and nieces Megan and Siân, have all been eagerly waiting for *Real Soups and Sauces*. In their student days and beyond, they are sure to find it becomes an indispensable book. I hope you do too.

Happy cooking!

Annette Yates

1

NOTES ABOUT THE RECIPES

For best results, use one set of measurements – metric or imperial. All spoon measurements are level, unless otherwise stated.

A word about stock:
In the recipes, where two types of stock are listed (for instance, I may suggest using chicken or vegetable stock), these are the ones I have tested, with my preference listed first. However, you will want to use the stock of your own choice (if you are a vegetarian, for example, you will not want to use chicken stock). The result may be different but it will be just as delicious.

Puréeing soups:
When puréeing soup in a food processor or liquidiser, you will probably need to do it in batches.

Adjusting the consistency of soups:
The consistency of the finished soup can vary slightly. Since ingredients, saucepans, hobs and microwaves vary, it is always a good idea to have some extra stock or liquid handy, so that you can thin the soup to the desired consistency if necessary.

Microwave instructions:
When a recipe is appropriate, and most are, microwave methods have been given. The recipes have been tested in a microwave oven with a wattage of 700-800W. If your microwave has a lower wattage, you will need to cook for a little longer. If it has a higher wattage, then simply lower the power level slightly and cook for the time given in the recipe. All cooking is on HIGH unless otherwise stated. MED-HIGH is equivalent to 500-600W, MEDIUM is 350-400W and MED-LOW is 200-300W.

You will notice that, when making soups, I use *hot* stock whenever possible (so if you make up a stock cube or granules, dissolve it in boiling water from the kettle then add it to the recipe).

Freezing:
When a recipe is suitable for freezing, I have indicated in the recipe. Always cool the soup or sauce and freeze it as soon as possible.

2

MAKING YOUR OWN STOCK

Stock is the basis of most soups and many savoury sauces. Making your own stock can be a rewarding pastime and there is no doubt that a good home-made stock produces a soup or a sauce with a flavour which is unique. So when time allows, or when you have the ingredients to hand, it's worth making up a large quantity. The portion that you don't use can be reduced by gentle boiling, and then cooled, and frozen in small blocks for a later date.

Cartons of fresh stock are available in the chilled cabinets of large supermarkets. Some of them are very good and they contain little salt, sugar or artificial additives.

What about stock cubes and granules? In my opinion, there is nothing wrong with using stock cubes if it means you are encouraged to make soups and sauces. They are all quick to use, though some are better than others. I use them and I am always on the look out for good products with light, well-balanced flavours (the ones I have discarded are those which are overpoweringly strong and very salty).

At the time this book is being written, we are not able to buy beef bones for making stock. The position could well have changed by the time you read this. In the meantime, I have found that an excellent alternative to a well-flavoured beef stock is a can of good-quality consommé, made up to the required amount with water if necessary. Alternatively, you could use a cube. New products appear on the market each day and one of the latest is a beef stock cube which is not derived from bones.

Vegetable Stock

This makes a light and delicate stock. Vegetables to use include onions, leeks, garlic, carrots, celery, celeriac, parsnips, cabbage, tomatoes and red or yellow peppers. Vegetable trimmings can be used too (including mushrooms, celery tops and tomato skins) as well as fresh herbs.

about 675g/1½ lb vegetables, washed, peel left on and roughly chopped
10 black peppercorns
1 small lemon, roughly chopped
bouquet garni (see TIP on page 15)
salt

1. Put the vegetables, peppercorns, lemon and bouquet garni into a large pan with 1.2 litre/2 pt cold water. Season lightly with salt.

2. Bring to the boil, skimming off any scum that rises to the surface (use a large spoon). Partially cover and simmer gently for about 45 minutes, occasionally removing any scum.

3. Strain through a fine sieve or a colander lined with muslin (before lining the colander, wet the muslin and wring out excess water).

4. If you plan to use the stock as it is, check the seasoning, adding salt and pepper to taste. If you plan to reduce the stock (for a more concentrated flavour), tip it into a saucepan and bring to the boil. Simmer gently, skimming the surface as necessary, until the stock has reduced by about half. Adjust the seasoning as required.

5. Use at once or cool and chill for up to 2 days.

To microwave:

1. Put the vegetables, peppercorns, lemon and bouquet garni into a large casserole with 1.2 litre/2 pt cold water. Season lightly with salt.

2. Cover and cook on HIGH for about 10 minutes or until the mixture comes to the boil, then cook on MED-LOW for 25-30 minutes.

3. As step 3 above.

4. If you plan to use the stock as it is, check the seasoning, adding salt and pepper to taste. If you plan to reduce the stock (for a more concentrated flavour), return it to the casserole and cook, uncovered, on HIGH for about 15 minutes or until the stock has reduced by about half. Adjust the seasoning if necessary.

5. As step 5 above.

Meat Stock

Use raw or cooked bones. Raw bones (ask your butcher to chop them into small pieces) can be browned in a hot oven first to make a richer, darker stock. Extra colour can be added by including the skin of the onion.

about 1kg/2¼ lb raw bones – ham, pork or lamb
1 onion, thickly sliced
1 carrot, thickly sliced
1 celery stick, thickly sliced
bouquet garni
10 black peppercorns
½ tsp salt

1. Put all the ingredients into a large pan and cover with cold water (about 1.7 litre/3 pt). Bring to the boil, skimming off any scum that rises to the surface (use a large spoon).

2. Partially cover and simmer gently for about 2 hours, occasionally removing any scum.

3. Strain through a colander lined with muslin (before lining the colander, wet the muslin and wring out excess water).

4. If you plan to use the stock as it is, check the seasoning, adding salt and pepper to taste. If you plan to reduce the stock (for a more concentrated flavour), tip it into a saucepan and bring to the boil. Simmer gently, skimming the surface as necessary, until the stock has reduced by about half. Adjust the seasoning as required.

5. Spoon off any fat from the surface, then cool and chill for up to 3 days.

To microwave:
1. Put all the ingredients into a large casserole with 1.2 litre/2 pt cold water. Season lightly with salt.

2. Cover and cook on HIGH for about 10 minutes or until the mixture comes to the boil, then cook on MED-LOW for about 1 hour, occasionally removing any scum.

3. As step 3 above.

4. If you plan to use the stock as it is, check the seasoning, adding salt and pepper to taste. If you plan to reduce the stock (for a more concentrated flavour), return it to the casserole and cook, uncovered, on HIGH for about 15 minutes or until the stock has reduced by about half. Adjust the seasoning if necessary.

5. As step 5 above.

TIP:

Instead of using a dried bouquet garni, why not make a fresh one? Tie together one or two bay leaves with some sprigs of parsley and thyme, rosemary or sage (use less of this – its flavour can come through strongly).

TIP:

A pressure cooker can reduce the cooking time of stock by about half. Follow the manufacturer's instructions.

Poultry or Game Stock

Raw bones are best but cooked carcasses produce good stock too. Making stock is a good way to get the most out of the Christmas turkey. For a golden colour, leave the skin on the onion. When making game stock, adding some cracked allspice or juniper berries gives an extra dimension to the flavour.

raw or cooked carcass, broken into pieces
1 onion, sliced
1 carrot, sliced
1 celery stick, sliced
few sprigs of herbs, such as tarragon and thyme
2 bay leaves
piece of fresh root ginger, peel left on and roughly chopped

1. Put all the ingredients into a large pan and cover with cold water (about 1.7 litre/3 pt). Bring to the boil, skimming off any scum that rises to the surface (use a large spoon).

2. Partially cover and simmer gently for about 2 hours, occasionally removing any scum.

3. Strain through a colander lined with muslin (before lining the colander, wet the muslin and wring out excess water).

4. If you plan to use the stock as it is, check the seasoning, adding salt and pepper to taste. If you plan to reduce the stock (for a more concentrated flavour), tip it into a saucepan and bring to the boil. Simmer gently, skimming the surface as necessary, until the stock has reduced by about half. Adjust the seasoning as required.

5. Spoon off any fat from the surface, then cool and chill for up to 3 days.

To microwave:

1. Put all the ingredients into a large casserole with 1.2 litre/2 pt cold water. Season lightly with salt.

2. Cover and cook on HIGH for about 10 minutes or until the mixture comes to the boil, then cook on MED-LOW for about 45 minutes, occasionally removing any scum.

3. As step 3 above.

4. If you plan to use the stock as it is, check the seasoning, adding salt and pepper to taste. If you plan to reduce the stock (for a more concentrated flavour), return it to the casserole and cook, uncovered, on HIGH for about 15 minutes or until the stock has reduced by about half. Adjust the seasoning if necessary.

5. As step 5 above.

Fish Stock

Home-made fish stock has wonderfully delicate flavour. The best
fish for stock-making is white fish such as plaice, cod, haddock,
hake, sole, turbot and whiting. For a slight smoky flavour, add a
small piece of smoked haddock or cod. For a good colour, leave the
skin on the onion.

about 1kg/2¼ lb fish bones, heads and trimmings
300ml/½ pt white wine
1 onion, sliced
1 carrot, sliced
1 small lemon, roughly chopped
2-3 parsley sprigs
2-3 fennel sprigs
2 bay leaves
10 black peppercorns
2 tsp sugar

1. Put all the ingredients into a large pan with 1 litre/1¾ pt cold
   water. Bring to the boil, skimming off any scum that rises to the
   surface (use a large spoon).

2. Partially cover and simmer gently for about 20 minutes, occasionally removing any scum.

3. Strain through a colander lined with muslin (before lining the
   colander, wet the muslin and wring out excess water).

4. If you plan to use the stock as it is, check the seasoning, adding
   salt and pepper to taste. If you plan to reduce the stock (for a more
   concentrated flavour), tip it into a saucepan and bring to the boil.
   Simmer gently, skimming the surface as necessary, until the stock
   has reduced by about half. Adjust the seasoning as required.

5. Use at once or cool and chill for up to 2 days.

To microwave:

1. Put all the ingredients into a large casserole with 600ml/1 pt cold water. Season lightly with salt.

2. Cover and cook on HIGH for about 10 minutes or until the mixture comes to the boil, then cook on MED-LOW for 10-15 minutes. Remove any scum.

3. As step 3 above.

4. If you plan to use the stock as it is, check the seasoning, adding salt and pepper to taste. If you plan to reduce the stock (for a more concentrated flavour), return it to the casserole and cook, uncovered, on HIGH for about 10 minutes or until the stock has reduced by about half. Adjust the seasoning if necessary.

5. As step 5 above.

3

GARNISHES AND ACCOMPANIMENTS

Hot or chilled, a soup can be transformed by a simple garnish. Though a garnish is essentially a decoration (adding colour, contrast and shape) it can also add texture, flavour, body and interest to a soup. In other words, it livens things up!

Simply ladle the soup into serving bowls and add the garnish. Alternatively, serve one or more garnishes in separate bowls and pass them round the table for your guests to help themselves. Here are some ideas to get you started.

- **Fresh herbs** – small sprigs, leaves or chopped. Choose herbs which will complement the soup. Try parsley, mint, chives, coriander, basil, tarragon, chervil or dill, or a mixture.
- **Crisp-fried herbs** – sage leaves and parsley sprigs are best, washed, dried and lightly fried in butter or oil until just crisp.
- **Fresh edible flowers** – herb flowers in particular look pretty and taste good.
- **Cream, yogurt, fromage frais or crème fraîche** – swirl a spoonful on top of the soup. A sprinkling of chopped fresh herbs looks good over it too.
- **Croûtons** – see how to make them on page 23.
- **Lemon, orange or lime** slices. Shreds of citrus zest look and taste good too. Pour boiling water over them and leave to stand while you make the soup. Just before serving drain and scatter a few shreds on top of each serving.
- **Vegetables** – raw or blanched, they add colour and crunch. Try raw cucumber slices, chopped tomato (skin and seeds removed), or small sprigs of watercress. Or what about blanched carrot strips, fresh peas or asparagus?
- **Crisp-fried vegetables** – add extra flavour as well as colour and

texture. Try thin onion rings, whole baby mushrooms; strips of leek, parsnip, or carrot; or wafer-thin slices (crisps) of potato, sweet potato, beetroot.

- **Cheese** – freshly grated or shaved Parmesan and Cheddar are probably the best, but do try others (grated or cut into tiny cubes) that complement the ingredients of the soup.
- **Crispy bacon** – small pieces of bacon, fried or grilled until crisp and crumbly. Remember that bacon is usually quite salty, so make sure that the soup isn't.
- **Rice, pasta and other grains** – adding these makes a soup into a more substantial snack or meal, and it's a good way of using leftovers. Just before serving the soup, add some cooked rice or pasta shapes – add it hot to each serving bowl, or stir it into the main body of the soup and heat through before serving. Cooked grains, like couscous and bulgar wheat are ideal for using this way too.
- **Nuts and seeds** – almond flakes, hazelnuts, pistachios and pine nuts are each delicious, fried or toasted. Try toasted seeds, like sesame, sunflower, melon, or fennel.
- **Toasted coconut** – is good served with spicy soups. Lightly toasted shavings work better than desiccated.

The ideal accompaniment to soup is often a hunk of good, fresh (preferably warm) crusty bread. Bakers and supermarkets now sell a huge range. For a change, why not choose from these?

- Flavoured bread, such as cheese, tomato or olive.
- Soda bread.
- Italian-style breads containing olive oil, such as ciabatta or focaccia.
- Pizza – either make your own or buy a ready-made pizza base, brush it with plain, garlic or herb butter and grill until crisp and golden.
- Italian bread sticks – buy them plain or flavoured.
- Bruschetta – recipe on page 26.
- Indian breads, such as naan or chappaties, grilled or baked in the oven.
- Samosas, filled with spicy vegetables and cooked until crisp.
- Filo parcels, filled with cheese (feta or ricotta is good) and chopped fresh herbs, then fried or oven-cooked until crisp and golden.
- Chinese spring rolls – crisply fried.

- Muffins – split and toasted.
- Potato pancakes.
- Freshly-baked scones – plain, herb or cheese.
- Croûtes – bread slices, baked in the oven until crisp (see page 23).
- Cheesy toasts or croûtes – small pieces of thickly-sliced fresh bread, topped with grated cheese and grilled (try Parmesan, Cheddar or Gruyère).
- Hot garlic bread – recipe on page 24.
- Hot herb bread – recipe on page 24.
- Melba toast is ideal for serving with a light soup at the start of an elegant meal – see how to make it on page 25.
- Cheese sticks – recipe on page 25.
- Dumplings – see Cock-a-Leekie with Mini Dumplings on page 104.

Croûtons

Use stale, firm-textured bread to make croûtons.

To fry:
Remove the crusts and cut the bread into small cubes. In a pan, heat some butter or oil until hot, add the bread and cook, stirring gently, until crisp and golden brown. Drain on absorbent kitchen paper. Once cooked and cooled, these croûtons can be kept in a sealed container for up to one week.

To toast:
Remove the crusts from the bread slices. Toast the bread on both sides and cut into cubes. Serve immediately.

To microwave:
Thinly spread both sides of two bread slices with butter (alternatively, brush lightly with olive oil) and remove the crusts. Cut the bread into 1cm/½ in cubes. Spread the cubes in an even layer on a heatproof plate. Cook, uncovered on MED-HIGH for about 2-3 minutes, stirring once or twice, until they just start to brown. The croûtons will continue to crisp up on cooling. These are best used on the day they are made.

Garlic Croûtons

If you are frying croûtons, add some slices of garlic to the cooking fat as it heats up, lifting it out when it begins to turn brown. When toasting, try rubbing the bread with a split garlic clove before putting it under the grill. Alternatively, add some finely-chopped or crushed garlic to the butter or oil before spreading it on the bread.

Parmesan Croûtons

Sprinkle some freshly grated Parmesan cheese over the freshly-cooked, still-hot croûtons.

Croûtes

Croûtes are crisp and crunchy – ideal for serving with soup. Cut a small French baguette into 1cm/½ in slices. Lightly brush both sides of each slice with melted butter. Arrange them on a baking sheet and cook at 180°C/350°F/Gas Mark 4 for about 10 minutes, turning them over once, or until crisp and golden brown.

Hot Garlic Bread

This method uses a French stick, but I have made Garlic Bread from all shapes and types of loaves.

Serves 8-10

1 large French stick
115g/4 oz soft butter
4 plump garlic cloves, crushed or finely chopped

1. Make diagonal cuts into the bread, about 2.5cm/1 in apart, without quite slicing it right through.

2. Mix together the butter and garlic and spread the mixture between the slices and, lastly, over the top of the loaf.

3. Wrap loosely in foil, put into a preheated oven and cook at 200°C/400°F/Gas Mark 6 for about 10 minutes.

Hot Herb Bread

Follow the recipe for Hot Garlic Bread, omitting the garlic and adding 2-4 tbsp chopped fresh herbs – try parsley, thyme, chives, coriander, or a mixture. If you like, add a little finely-grated lemon rind too.

Melba Toast

Use stale bread for best results. Once cooled, Melba Toast can be stored in an airtight container for several days. Serve it with or without butter.

1. Using a grill or toaster, toast some bread slices on both sides until golden brown.

2. Cut off the crusts then, holding the toast flat, cut it horizontally into two thin slices. Cut each slice into 4 triangles.

3. Arrange the pieces, toasted-side down, on a grill pan. Toast until the edges curl and the toast is golden brown.

4. Serve warm or leave to cool on a rack.

Cheese Sticks

Stored in an airtight container, these can be kept for up to one week.

Makes about 20

375g ready-rolled puff pastry, thawed if frozen
1 small egg, beaten
85g/3 oz freshly grated Parmesan cheese

1. Unroll the pastry and, using a sharp knife, trim off all the edges. Brush the pastry with beaten egg and sprinkle the cheese evenly over the top. Halve the pastry lengthways, then cut crossways to make about 20 strips.

2. Arrange on a baking sheet, separating them slightly. Put into a preheated oven and cook at 180°C/350°F/Gas Mark 4 for about 15 minutes or until puffed, misshapen and golden brown.

3. Cool on a wire rack.

Bruschetta

Use extra virgin olive oil for the best flavour.

Serves 6

6 large slices of country-style bread, such as ciabatta
1 plump garlic clove
olive oil

1. Toast the bread until both sides are crisp and quite hard.

2. Halve the garlic clove and rub the cut sides over the bread (the idea is that the juice of the garlic is absorbed into the bread). Drizzle one side of each bread slice generously with olive oil.

3. Leave to stand for 5 minutes, then serve.

Goats' Cheese Crostini

These are particularly good served with vegetable soups.

Toast thick slices of French bread on one side. On the untoasted side, put a slice of chèvre or other goats' cheese and grill until bubbling. Serve immediately.

SOUPS

There is nothing quite like a real home-made soup. Whether it's a chilly winter's evening or a warm summer's day, whether it begins the meal as a starter or is a meal in itself, whether it's a casual snack or a formal dinner, there is one to suit every occasion. A soup can be delicate or assertive, smooth or chunky, thin or thick, clear or creamy, light or filling – you, the cook, are the one who decides.

For ease of use, I have grouped the recipes into sections. However, if for instance there is a main-meal soup that you would like to serve in small portions as a starter, then do it. The choice is yours – go mad!

4

LIGHT SOUPS AND SOUPS FOR A SUMMER'S DAY

Here is a collection of soups which are ideal for serving at the start of a meal. Some are more delicately flavoured than others, but none of them should spoil you for the rest of the meal.

Several of the soups are ideal for serving chilled – wonderfully refreshing and cooling on a warm summer's day. When you really need to cool down, place one or two ice cubes in each serving bowl before ladling in the chilled soup. Though I have chosen to group these soups together as 'light', you will find that many of them are just as good served hot at any time of the year. A few need no cooking at all – they are simply made from fresh ingredients, whizzed up in the food processor or liquidiser.

Clear Vegetable Soup

For a more substantial affair, add some tiny dumplings with the tomatoes and peas in step 2. Cover the soup while the dumplings cook. For dumplings, see page 104.

Serves 4-6

1 litre/1¾ pt vegetable stock
2 medium carrots, cut into small dice
1 small leek, thinly sliced
2 small celery sticks, thinly sliced
350g/12 oz tomatoes, skinned, seeds removed and chopped
115g/4 oz frozen petit pois
salt and freshly milled pepper
2 tbsp chopped fresh parsley

1. Put the stock into a pan and bring to the boil. Add the carrots, leek and celery and simmer gently for about 5 minutes or until the vegetables are just soft.

2. Stir in the tomatoes and peas and simmer gently for 2-3 minutes.

3. Season to taste, stir in the parsley and serve.

To microwave:
1. Put half the *hot* stock into a casserole and cook on HIGH for about 5 minutes or until it just comes to the boil. Stir in the carrots, leek and celery, cover and cook on HIGH for about 5 minutes or until the vegetables are just soft.

2. Add the tomatoes and peas and cook on HIGH for 2 minutes. Stir in the remaining *hot* stock.

3. Season to taste, stir in the parsley and serve.

TIP:

To skin fresh tomatoes, see page 35.

Watercress and Orange Soup

This looks beautiful garnished with thin strips of orange peel (cooked in boiling water for 2-3 minutes until tender). For traditional watercress soup, use chicken stock and omit the orange.

Serves 6

2 bunches of watercress
25g/1 oz butter
1 medium onion, finely chopped
1 medium main-crop potato, cut into small pieces
850ml/1½ pt chicken or vegetable stock
salt and freshly milled pepper
300ml/½ pt milk
1 medium orange

To serve:
single cream

1. Reserve a few sprigs of watercress for garnish then roughly chop the rest.

2. Melt the butter in a pan, add the onion and cook gently for about 5 minutes, stirring occasionally, until soft but not brown.

3. Stir in the watercress and potato. Add the stock and season with salt and pepper. Bring to the boil then simmer gently for about 15 minutes until the potato is very soft.

4. Leave to cool slightly then add the milk. Tip into a food processor or liquidiser and purée until smooth. Return the soup to the pan.

5. Finely grate half the rind from the orange and squeeze the juice from both halves. Add to the pan and adjust the seasoning if necessary.

6. Reheat gently. Serve each bowl with a little cream spooned over the top and garnish with the reserved watercress.

To microwave:

1. As step 1 above.

2. Put the butter and onion into a large casserole and cook on HIGH for about 3 minutes until soft.

3. Stir in the watercress and potato. Add half the *hot* stock and season with salt and pepper. Cover and cook on HIGH for about 10 minutes or until the potato is very soft.

4. Add the remaining stock, then continue as steps 4-6 above.

TIP:

This soup is also good served chilled.

Lettuce and Petit Pois Soup

This recipe is ideal for using up lettuce that is beginning to bolt in the summer garden. If you can replace the frozen peas with fresh young garden peas, so much the better.

Serves 4

25g/1 oz butter
2 shallots, finely chopped
225g/8 oz lettuce leaves, shredded
175g/6 oz frozen petit pois
1 tbsp flour
700ml/1¼ pt vegetable stock
salt and freshly milled pepper
200g carton crème fraîche
2 tbsp chopped fresh herbs, such as mint, parsley or coriander

1. Melt the butter in a pan, add the shallots and cook gently for 2-3 minutes until soft but not brown.

2. Stir in the lettuce and petit pois and cook gently for 2-3 minutes, stirring, until the lettuce has wilted. Stir in the flour, then gradually add the stock. Bring to the boil, stirring, then cover and simmer gently for about 10 minutes.

3. Leave to cool slightly, then tip into a food processor or liquidiser and purée until smooth. Season to taste.

4. Stir in the crème fraîche and herbs. Reheat gently and serve.

To microwave

1. Put the butter and shallots into a large casserole, cover and cook on HIGH for 2 minutes until soft.

2. Stir in the lettuce and petit pois and cook on HIGH for 2 minutes until the lettuce has wilted. Stir in the flour, then gradually add the stock. Cook on HIGH for about 5 minutes, stirring occasionally, until the mixture comes to the boil. Cover and cook on MEDIUM for about 10 minutes.

3. Continue steps 3-4 as above.

To freeze:

Cool and freeze at the end of step 3. Reheat and complete step 4.

Herbed Tomato with Rice

This recipe is just as good when the rice is replaced with fine vermicelli.

Serves 6

1 tbsp olive oil
1 medium onion, finely chopped
1 plump garlic clove, finely chopped
400g can chopped tomatoes
850ml/1½ pt vegetable stock
2 tsp dried oregano, or 1½ tbsp chopped fresh
1 tbsp sugar
salt and freshly milled pepper
50g/1¾ oz long grain rice
4 medium tomatoes, skinned, seeds removed and chopped

1. Put the oil, onion and garlic into a pan and cook gently for about 5 minutes, stirring occasionally, until soft but not brown.

2. Stir in the canned tomatoes, stock, oregano and sugar. Bring to the boil, then cover and simmer gently for about 10 minutes. Season to taste with salt and pepper.

3. Leave to cool slightly, then tip the mixture into a food processor or liquidiser and purée until smooth.

4. Return the puréed mixture to the pan and stir in the rice. Bring to the boil, then simmer gently for about 10 minutes or until the rice is just tender.

5. Stir in the fresh tomatoes, adjust the seasoning if necessary and serve.

To microwave:

1. Put the oil, onion and garlic into a large casserole. Cook on HIGH for about 3 minutes until soft.

2. Stir in the canned tomatoes, half the *hot* stock, oregano and sugar. Cover and cook on HIGH for about 5 minutes, stirring once. Add the remaining stock and season with salt and pepper.

3. As step 3 above.

4. Return the puréed mixture to the casserole and stir in the rice. Cook, uncovered, on HIGH for about 10 minutes or until the rice is just tender.

5. Stir in the fresh tomatoes, adjust the seasoning if necessary and serve.

To freeze:

Cool and freeze at the end of step 3. Reheat the soup and continue as steps 4-5 above.

TIP:

To skin fresh tomatoes, pour over sufficient boiling water to cover them and leave to stand for 5 minutes. Drain them and the skins will peel off easily.

Clear Chicken and Tomato Soup

A lightly flavoured soup which makes an ideal start to a meal. The egg whites help to keep the broth clear.

Serves 4

1 litre/1¾ pt chicken stock
1 medium onion, finely chopped
2 garlic cloves, halved
2 medium carrots, finely chopped
2 celery sticks, finely chopped
400g can chopped tomatoes
4 boneless chicken thighs, skin and fat removed
2 egg whites
salt and freshly milled pepper
1 tbsp dry sherry (optional)

1. Put the stock in a pan and add the onion, garlic, carrots, celery, tomatoes (including their juice) and chicken. Whisk the egg whites until frothy and add to the pan.
2. Heat gently, whisking continually, until a thick frothy sludge starts to form on the surface. Stop whisking and continue heating until the mixture just comes to the boil. Immediately reduce the heat and simmer very gently for about 30 minutes.
3. Line a sieve with muslin and sit it over a large bowl. Carefully pour the mixture into the sieve, gently holding the top layer back and then finally allowing it to slide into the sieve.
4. Lift the chicken pieces from the sieve, rinse and dry on kitchen paper. Cut the chicken into small strips.
5. Pour the strained liquid into a clean pan, reheat gently (until not quite boiling), season to taste and stir in the sherry (if using).
6. Spoon the chicken pieces into the bottom of warmed bowls and pour the soup over.

TIP:

During cooking, the vegetables and egg white will sit on the top, acting as a filter which will clarify the soup. If cooking is too quick, the surface will break, causing the soup to be cloudy.

Beef Consommé with Ginger

In the absence of a well-flavoured beef stock, use a can of good-quality consommé, topped up with water to make the required amount. For a more traditional flavour, replace the ginger with a bouquet garni.

Serves 4-6

1.2 litre/2 pt beef stock
115g/4 oz lean rump steak
2 medium onions, roughly chopped
2 medium carrots, roughly chopped
2 celery sticks, roughly chopped
large piece of root ginger, finely chopped
2 egg whites
salt and freshly milled pepper

1. Put the stock in a large pan and add the steak, vegetables and ginger. Whisk the egg whites until frothy and add to the pan.

2. Heat gently, whisking continually, until a thick frothy sludge starts to form on the surface. Stop whisking and continue heating until the mixture just comes to the boil. Immediately reduce the heat and simmer very gently for about 30 minutes.

3. Line a sieve with muslin and sit it over a large bowl. Carefully pour the mixture into the sieve, gently holding the top layer back and then finally allowing it to slide into the sieve.

4. Tip the clear liquid into a clean pan and reheat gently until almost, but not quite, boiling.

5. Season to taste and serve.

TIP:

When making clear soups, make sure the ingredients and the utensils are free from fat.

French Onion Soup

This soup traditionally has slices of cheese-topped French bread floating on the top. To lighten it up, you could serve it instead with some tiny Parmesan Croûtons (see page 23).

Serves 4

25g/1 oz butter
450g/1 lb onions, thinly sliced in rings
1 tsp sugar
2 tbsp cornflour
1 litre/1¾ pt beef stock
salt and freshly milled pepper

To serve:
4 French bread slices
50g/1¾ oz Gruyère or Cheddar cheese, grated

1. Melt the butter in a pan, add the onions and sugar and cook gently for about 15 minutes, stirring occasionally, until very soft and light golden brown.

2. Stir in the cornflour, then gradually stir in the stock. Season with salt and pepper.

3. Bring to the boil, stirring continuously, until the soup thickens slightly. Cover and simmer gently for about 30 minutes.

4. Top the bread slices with cheese and grill until bubbling and golden. Float one slice on top of each serving of soup. Alternatively, ladle the soup into flameproof dishes, float the cheese-topped bread on top and put under a hot grill until bubbling and golden.

To microwave:

1. Put the butter, onions and sugar into a large casserole, cover and cook on HIGH for about 5 minutes, stirring once, until soft.

2. Stir in the cornflour, then gradually stir in the *hot* stock. Season with salt and pepper.

3. Cook on HIGH for about 5 minutes, stirring occasionally, or until the soup comes to the boil and thickens slightly. Cover and cook on MEDIUM for about 15 minutes.

4. Continue as step 4 above.

To freeze:
Cool and freeze at the end of step 3. Reheat and continue with step 4.

TIP:

Try adding a good dash of Worcestershire sauce with the stock in step 2.

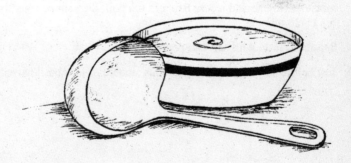

Roasted Plum Tomato Soup

If you cannot get plum tomatoes, use any ripe variety. Good served with freshly baked or toasted Italian bread such as Ciabatta.

Serves 4

900g/2 lb ripe plum tomatoes, halved lengthways
3 tbsp olive oil
2 plump garlic cloves, finely chopped
2 tbsp chopped fresh thyme leaves, or 1 tbsp dried
850ml/1½ pt chicken or vegetable stock
salt and freshly milled pepper
fresh basil leaves

1. Arrange the tomatoes, cut side up, on a baking sheet. Drizzle over 2 tbsp olive oil. Put into a preheated oven, at 200°C/400°F/Gas Mark 6, for about 45 minutes or until the tomatoes are brown and soft.

2. Tip the tomatoes, with any juices, into a food processor or liquidiser and blend until slightly chunky. (If you prefer a very smooth soup, purée for longer then pass it through a fine nylon sieve.)

3. Heat the remaining 1 tbsp oil in a large pan and add the garlic, cooking gently for 1-2 minutes without browning it. Stir in the tomatoes, thyme and stock. Bring to the boil, then simmer gently for 15-20 minutes.

4. Season to taste with salt and pepper.

5. Just before serving, stir in a generous amount of torn basil leaves.

To microwave:

1. As step 1 above.

2. As step 2 above.

3. Put the remaining 1 tbsp oil into a large casserole. Stir in the garlic and cook on HIGH for 20 seconds. Add the tomatoes, thyme and half the *hot* stock. Cover and cook on HIGH for about 10 minutes.

4. Stir in the remaining stock and continue as steps 4 and 5 above.

To freeze:

Cool and freeze at the end of step 4.

Shallot and Spinach Soup

No fresh spinach? Use 175g/6 oz frozen spinach leaves instead.

Serves 4-6

25g/1 oz butter
225g/8 oz shallots
1 medium main-crop potato, thinly sliced
850ml/1½ pt chicken or vegetable stock
salt and freshly milled pepper
225g/8 oz fresh spinach leaves, shredded
good pinch of freshly grated nutmeg
2 tbsp double cream

1. Melt the butter in a pan, add the shallots and cook gently for about 5 minutes, stirring occasionally, until soft but not brown.

2. Stir in the potato, stock and seasoning. Bring to the boil, cover and simmer gently for about 15 minutes, until the potato is very soft.

3. Add the spinach and nutmeg, bring to the boil, then simmer gently for 5 minutes.

4. Leave to cool slightly, then tip into a food processor or liquidiser and purée until smooth.

5. Reheat, adjusting the seasoning if necessary. Stir in the cream and serve.

To microwave:
1. Put the butter and shallots into a large casserole. Cover and cook on HIGH for about 3 minutes or until soft.

2. Stir in the potato, half the *hot* stock and seasoning. Cook on HIGH for about 10 minutes, stirring once or twice, or until the potato is very soft.

3. Add the spinach and nutmeg, Cover and cook on HIGH for 5 minutes, stirring once.

4. Stir in the remaining stock and continue as steps 4-5 above.

To freeze:
Cool and freeze at the end of step 4. Thaw, then continue with step 5.

Minted Pea Soup

Make this delightful soup in minutes from a handful or two of frozen peas. This version is chilled, but it is good served hot too.

Serves 4-6

8 spring onions, sliced
175g/6 oz frozen peas
175g/6 oz main-crop potatoes, thinly sliced
425ml/¾ pt vegetable stock
425ml/¾ pt milk
2 tsp concentrated mint sauce
salt and freshly milled pepper

To serve:
150ml/¼ pt Greek-style yogurt
chopped chives

1. Put the onions, peas, potatoes and stock into a pan. Bring to the boil, then cover and simmer gently for about 15 minutes, or until the vegetables are very soft.

2. Leave to cool slightly, then tip into a food processor or liquidiser and purée until smooth. Add the milk and mint sauce and purée again. Season to taste.

3. Cool, cover and chill for several hours.

4. Just before serving, lightly stir in the yogurt. Serve sprinkled with chives.

To microwave:
1. Put the onions, peas, potatoes and *hot* stock into a large casserole. Cover and cook on HIGH for about 12 minutes, stirring once, or until the vegetables are soft.

2. Complete steps 2-4 as above.

To freeze:
Cool and freeze at the end of step 2.

Vichyssoise

A delicious chilled soup. To achieve the traditional pale colour of Vichyssoise, only the white parts of the leeks are used – so when you are buying them, choose young specimens with large areas of white.

Serves 6

25g/1 oz butter
450g/1 lb leeks, whites only, thinly sliced
1 medium onion, chopped
350g/12 oz main-crop potatoes, thinly sliced
700ml/1¼ pt chicken stock or vegetable stock
salt and freshly milled pepper
300ml/½ pt milk
150ml/¼ pt single cream
snipped chives, to garnish

1. Melt the butter in a pan, add the leeks and onion and cook gently for 8-10 minutes, stirring occasionally, until soft but not brown.

2. Add the potatoes, stock and seasoning. Bring to the boil, cover and simmer gently for 20-30 minutes until the vegetables are very soft.

3. Remove from the heat and stir in the milk.

4. Tip into a food processor or liquidiser and purée until smooth. For a really smooth result, pass the soup through a fine nylon sieve.

5. Leave to cool completely, stir in the cream and chill.

6. Serve garnished with chives.

To microwave:

1. Put the butter, leeks and onion into a large casserole, cover and cook on HIGH for 5 minutes, stirring once, until soft.

2. Add the potatoes, half the *hot* stock and seasoning. Cover and cook on HIGH for about 15 minutes, stirring occasionally, until the vegetables are very soft.

3. Stir in the remaining *hot* stock and then the milk.

4. Continue as steps 4-6 above.

Not suitable for freezing.

Gazpacho

No cooking here! This is a soup made from fresh salad ingredients and thickened with breadcrumbs. Serve it with crisp croûtons and extra vegetables (tomatoes, cucumber, pepper and onions – all cut into tiny pieces).

Serves 4-6

700g/1½ lb ripe tomatoes, skinned, seeds removed and chopped
1 small cucumber, skin and seeds removed and chopped
1 green or red pepper, seeds removed and chopped
6 spring onions, thinly sliced
2 plump garlic cloves, crushed
2 tbsp olive oil
2 tbsp red or white wine vinegar
115g/4 oz fresh white breadcrumbs
1 tsp sugar
salt and freshly milled pepper
600ml/1 pt cold chicken stock, plus extra if necessary

1. Put the tomatoes into a large bowl and add the cucumber, pepper, onions, garlic, oil, vinegar, breadcrumbs and sugar. Season with salt and pepper and mix well. Leave to stand for 10 minutes, stirring once or twice.

2. Stir in the cold stock. Tip into a food processor or liquidiser and purée until smooth. If necessary, add extra stock until the consistency is right for serving.

3. Chill for 2 hours or more.

TIP:

To skin fresh tomatoes, see page 35.

Chilled Beetroot Soup

If the occasion suits, add a splash of vodka just before serving.

Serves 4-6

1kg/2¼ lb beetroot
1 large onion, finely chopped
1.2 litre/2 pt chicken or vegetable stock
salt and freshly milled pepper
1 tsp sugar
2 tbsp red or white wine vinegar

To serve:
soured cream or thick natural yogurt
snipped chives

1. Peel and coarsely grate the beetroot. Put into a pan and add the onion and stock. Season with salt and pepper and the sugar.

2. Bring to the boil, then cover and simmer gently for about 45 minutes.

3. Strain, discarding the vegetables. Stir the vinegar into the soup and adjust the seasoning to taste.

4. Chill until ready to serve. To each bowl of soup, add a generous spoonful of cream or yogurt and some chives.

To microwave:
1. Peel and coarsely grate the beetroot. Put into a large casserole and add the onion and half the *hot* stock. Season with salt and pepper and the sugar.

2. Cover and cook on HIGH for about 5 minutes or until the mixture comes to the boil. Continue cooking on MEDIUM for about 20 minutes.

3. Stir in the remaining stock, leave to stand for 5-10 minutes, then continue as steps 3-4 above.

Asparagus Soup with Egg

This recipe is ideal for using older, more woody asparagus – because you can use the whole stalks. Eggs go well with asparagus, but you can of course serve the soup just as it is.

Serves 4

450g/1 lb asparagus
50g/1¾ oz butter
1 large onion, finely chopped
1 litre/1¾ pt vegetable stock
salt and freshly milled pepper
150ml/¼ pt Greek-style natural yogurt
4 small eggs, hard boiled

1. Cut the heads off the asparagus. Cook them in gently simmering water for about 3 minutes, or until only just tender. Drain, cool, cover and refrigerate.

2. Chop the asparagus stalks. Melt the butter in a pan, add the asparagus stalks and onion. Cook gently for about 5 minutes, stirring occasionally, until soft but not brown.

3. Add the stock and seasoning. Bring to the boil, then cover and simmer gently for about 30 minutes until the asparagus is very soft.

4. Leave to cool slightly, then tip into a food processor or liquidiser and purée until smooth. Pass the mixture through a fine nylon sieve to remove any stringy bits. Leave to cool.

5. Stir in the yogurt and adjust the seasoning to taste. Chill until required.

6. Peel and quarter the eggs. Place four quarters in the bottom of each serving bowl, ladle the soup over them and top with the asparagus heads.

To microwave:

1. Cut the heads off the asparagus. Put them into a small casserole with 2 tbsp water. Cover and cook on HIGH for 2-3 minutes, or until only just tender. Drain, cool, cover and refrigerate.

2. Chop the asparagus stalks. Put the butter, asparagus stalks and onion into a large casserole. Cover and cook for about 5 minutes, stirring once, until soft.

3. Add half the *hot* stock and season with salt and pepper. Cover and cook on HIGH for about 15 minutes or until the asparagus is very soft.

4. Add the remaining stock and continue as steps 4-6 above.

TIP:

To make asparagus and ham soup, omit the eggs and replace the vegetable stock with a light ham stock. Place some slivers of smoked ham in the bottom of each bowl before adding the soup.

Cucumber and Mint Soup

Another recipe that needs no cooking, this looks pretty served in glass bowls with one or two ice cubes dropped in the bottom of each. Serve it with crisp savoury biscuits or Melba Toast (page 25).

Serves 6

2 medium cucumbers
6 spring onions, sliced
15g/½ oz fresh mint leaves, plus extra to garnish
600ml/1 pt chicken stock (cold)
1 tsp sugar
1 tbsp white wine vinegar
150ml/¼ pt double cream
150ml/¼ pt thick Greek-style natural yogurt
salt and freshly milled pepper

1. Top and tail the cucumbers and halve lengthways. Scoop out and discard the seeds and roughly chop the flesh.

2. Put the chopped cucumber into a food processor or liquidiser. Add the onions, mint, stock, sugar and vinegar. Purée until very smooth.

3. Transfer the mixture to a large bowl and gently whisk in the cream and yogurt. Season to taste with salt and pepper.

4. Chill until required. Serve garnished with mint leaves.

Sorrel and Spinach Soup

Sorrel leaves have a lovely, fresh, lemony flavour. It is easily grown in the garden. If you can't get it, use entirely spinach.

Serves 4-6

25g/1 oz butter
1 medium onion, finely chopped
1 medium main-crop potato, thinly sliced
850ml/1½ pt vegetable or chicken stock
salt and freshly milled pepper
175g/6 oz sorrel leaves, coarsely shredded
175g/6 oz spinach leaves, coarsely shredded
2 tbsp double cream, plus extra for garnish

1. Melt the butter in a pan and add the onion. Cook gently for about 5 minutes, stirring occasionally, until soft but not brown.

2. Add the potato, stock and seasoning. Bring to the boil, cover and simmer gently for about 15 minutes or until the potato is tender.

3. Stir in the sorrel and spinach and simmer gently for about 5 minutes.

4. Leave to cool slightly, then tip into a food processor or liquidiser and purée until smooth.

5. Adjust the seasoning to taste, reheat and stir in the cream.

6. Serve with a small swirl of extra cream in each bowl.

To microwave:
1. Put the butter and onion into a casserole, cover and cook on HIGH for about 3 minutes or until soft.

2. Add the potato, half the *hot* stock and the seasoning. Cook on HIGH for about 10 minutes, stirring once or twice, or until the potato is very soft.

3. Stir in the sorrel and spinach, cover and cook on HIGH for 3 minutes.

4. Add the remaining stock and continue as steps 4-6.

To freeze:
Cool and freeze at the end of step 4. Thaw, then continue with steps 5 and 6.

Mussel Soup with Coconut and Coriander

Serve with plenty of warm crusty bread to mop up the fragrant juices. When cleaning the mussels, remember to discard any which are broken or which do not close when given a sharp tap.

Serves 4

25g/1 oz soft butter
25g/1 oz plain flour
150ml/¼ pt dry white wine
2 plump garlic cloves, finely chopped
1 piece of lemon grass, finely chopped (see TIP) (optional)
450g/1 lb small mussels, scrubbed and beards removed
600ml/1 pt fish or vegetable stock
200ml carton coconut cream
salt and freshly milled pepper
4 tbsp chopped fresh coriander

1. Using a fork, work the flour into the butter until well blended. Leave on one side.

2. Put the wine, garlic and lemon grass (if using) into a pan and bring to the boil. Add the mussels, cover and cook on a high heat for about 2 minutes, shaking the pan occasionally, until all the shells have opened.

3. With a slotted spoon, transfer the mussels to a bowl. Remove the mussels from their shells, leaving about 12 intact and discarding any which have not opened.

4. Strain the pan juices through a fine sieve and return them to the pan. Add the stock, coconut cream and seasoning. Bring to the boil, then simmer gently for 2-3 minutes.

5. Add the flour-and-butter mixture, one small piece at a time and stirring with a whisk, until the soup has thickened.

6. Return the mussels to the pan, including the 12 in their shells. Adjust the seasoning to taste and add the coriander. Heat through and serve.

To microwave:

1. As step 1 above.

2. Put the wine, garlic and lemon grass into a large casserole. Cook on HIGH for 45 seconds. Stir in the mussels, cover and cook on HIGH for about 4 minutes, stirring once, or until all the mussels have opened.

3. As step 3 above.

4. Strain the pan juices through a fine sieve and return them to the casserole. Add the stock, coconut cream and seasoning. Cook on HIGH for about 5 minutes or until the mixture comes to the boil.

5. Continue as steps 5 and 6 above, heating through until the soup comes to the boil.

Not suitable for freezing.

TIP:

Look out for those handy small jars of fresh lemon grass and herbs packed in oil. Once opened they will keep, refrigerated, for up to six weeks.

Spiced Courgette Soup

Recipe on page 72. I could not decide which section should include this soup, so I have put it into two.

Avocado and Spring Onion Soup

Try adding a splash of dry white wine to the chilled soup, just before serving.

Serves 4

1 bunch of spring onions
2 ripe avocados
finely grated rind and juice of 1 small lemon
150ml/¼ pt double cream
600ml/1 pt chicken or vegetable stock (cold)
salt and freshly milled pepper

1. Thinly slice the onions, reserving some of the green tops for garnish. Put them into a food processor or liquidiser.

2. Halve the avocados, remove the stones and spoon the flesh into the processor. Add the lemon rind and juice and purée until smooth. Add the cream and purée again.

3. Pass through a fine nylon sieve into a large bowl (this will remove any stringy bits). Gradually whisk in the cold stock. Season to taste. Chill until required.

4. Serve garnished with the spring onion tops.

5

PURÉED AND CREAMED SOUPS

Here are soups for occasions when a smooth puréed or creamy consistency is required. Perhaps you plan to serve them as a starter; perhaps you want a sophisticated soup which will look great with just a simple garnish of chopped herbs or a few tiny crisp croûtons. Perhaps, like my nephews, you just prefer smooth soups.

Two-Tomato Soup

For the best flavour, I like to use a combination of fresh and canned tomatoes. There's no need to skin the fresh tomatoes in this recipe. Don't be put off by the generous amount of sugar which is needed to season the soup – it's worth it!

Serves 4-6

15g/½ oz butter
1 tbsp olive oil
1 plump garlic clove, crushed or finely chopped
1 medium onion, finely chopped
450g/1 lb ripe tomatoes, quartered
400g can chopped tomatoes
2 tbsp tomato purée
1 tbsp sugar, plus extra as required (see step 4)
600ml/1 pt chicken or vegetable stock
1 tbsp chopped fresh herbs, such as thyme, oregano, basil and
    parsley
up to 600ml/1 pt milk
salt and freshly milled pepper

1. Put the butter, oil, garlic and onion into a pan and cook gently for about 5 minutes, stirring occasionally, until soft but not brown,

2. Add the fresh and canned tomatoes, tomato purée, sugar, stock and herbs. Bring to the boil, then cover and simmer gently for about 20 minutes.

3. Leave to cool slightly, then tip the mixture into a food processor or liquidiser and purée until smooth. Pass through a nylon sieve to remove seeds and skins.

4. Return the puréed soup to the pan. Add the milk and season to taste with salt and pepper. Stir in extra sugar until the soup is seasoned to your liking.

5. Reheat and serve.

To microwave:

1. Put the butter, oil, garlic and onion into a large casserole. Cover and cook on HIGH for about 3 minutes until soft.

2. Add the fresh and canned tomatoes, tomato purée, sugar, half the *hot* stock and the herbs. Cover and cook on HIGH for about 15 minutes, stirring once or twice.

3. Add the remaining stock, then continue as steps 3-5 above.

To freeze:
Cool and freeze at the end of step 4.

Sweetcorn Soup

A delicate yellow soup which is sure to please lovers of sweetcorn. It is nicest when served with croûtons.

Serves 4

25g/1 oz butter
1 medium onion, finely chopped
450g/1 lb frozen sweetcorn
600ml/1 pt chicken or vegetable stock
600ml/1 pt milk
salt and freshly milled pepper

To serve:
double cream (optional)
croûtons
chopped fresh parsley

1. Put the butter and onion into a pan and cook gently for about 5 minutes until soft but not brown.

2. Stir in the sweetcorn and stock. Bring to the boil, cover and simmer gently for about 20 minutes until the sweetcorn is very soft.

3. Leave to cool slightly, then tip the mixture into a food processor or liquidiser and purée until smooth. Pass through a nylon sieve, pressing the residue to squeeze out all the liquid. Return the liquid to the pan.

4. Tip the sweetcorn residue back into the processor or liquidiser and add the milk. Purée for a minute or two. Now pass this mixture through the sieve, again pressing it to squeeze out all the juice. Add the liquid to the pan and season to taste. Discard the residue.

5. Reheat gently and serve each bowl with a swirl of cream (if using), a spoonful of croûtons and some chopped parsley.

To microwave:

1. Put the butter and onion into a large casserole, cover and cook on HIGH for about 3 minutes until soft.

2. Stir in the sweetcorn and stock. Cover and cook on HIGH for about 15 minutes, stirring once, until the sweetcorn is very soft.

3. Continue as steps 3-5 above.

To freeze:
Cool and freeze at the end of step 4.

TIP:

To use canned sweetcorn in place of frozen, drain two 300g cans.

Mushroom and Sun-Dried Tomato Soup

Dried mushrooms and tomatoes give this soup a wonderfully-concentrated 'meaty' flavour.

Serves 4-6

50g/1¾ oz mixed dried mushrooms
25g/1 oz butter
1 medium onion, finely chopped
1 plump garlic clove, crushed
1 small carrot, finely chopped
850ml/1½ pt chicken stock
4-6 sun-dried tomatoes, cut into fine slivers
2 tbsp tomato purée (preferably sun-dried)
salt and freshly milled pepper
300ml/½ pt cream/milk
chopped fresh parsley, to garnish

1. Cover the mushrooms with 600ml/1 pt boiling water and leave to stand for 30 minutes, stirring occasionally. Drain the soaking liquid through a sieve lined with wet kitchen paper or muslin (to remove any grit) and reserve. Rinse the mushrooms (again, to remove grit), dry them and chop finely.

2. Melt the butter in a pan and add the onion, garlic and carrot. Cook gently for about 5 minutes, stirring occasionally, or until soft but not brown.

3. Add the mushrooms, mushroom liquid, stock, tomatoes and tomato purée. Season with pepper. Bring to the boil, cover and simmer gently for about 20 minutes.

4. Leave to cool slightly, then tip about two-thirds of the mixture into a food processor or liquidiser. Purée until smooth. Add the cream/milk and purée again.

5. Stir into the remaining mixture in the pan and season to taste. Reheat gently and serve garnished with parsley.

To microwave:
1. As step 1 above.

2. Put the butter, onion, garlic and carrot into a large casserole. Cover and cook on HIGH for about 3 minutes, stirring once, or until soft.

3. Add the mushrooms, mushroom liquid, half the *hot* stock, tomatoes and tomato purée. Season with pepper. Cook on HIGH for about 5 minutes or until the mixture comes to the boil. Cover and cook on MEDIUM for about 15 minutes.

4. Add the remaining stock, then continue as step 4 above.

5. As step 5 above.

To freeze:
Cool and freeze at the end of step 4.

TIP:

If you prefer your soup to be velvety smooth, purée the whole lot in step 4.

Spiced Parsnip and Potato Soup

This is based on a recipe given to me by my good friend, cookery writer Caroline Young.

Serves 4-6

1 tbsp oil
1 medium onion, thinly sliced
1 plump garlic clove, crushed
1 tbsp finely chopped fresh ginger root
1 tbsp curry paste
450g/1 lb parsnips, thinly sliced
225g/8 oz potatoes, thinly sliced
600ml/1 pt vegetable stock, plus extra if necessary
2 tbsp dried skimmed milk
salt and freshly milled pepper

To serve:
thick yogurt
chopped fresh coriander or mint

1. Put the oil, onion, garlic and ginger into a pan and cook gently for about 5 minutes, stirring occasionally, until soft but not brown. Add the curry paste and cook, stirring gently, for about 2 minutes.

2. Add the parsnips, potatoes and stock. Bring to the boil, then cover and simmer gently for about 20 minutes or until the parsnips are really soft.

3. Leave to cool slightly, then tip the mixture into a food processor or liquidiser and purée until smooth.

4. Add the dried milk and purée again.

5. Season to taste and, if necessary, add some extra stock or water until the soup is the required consistency.

6. Reheat and ladle into warm bowls, topping each one with a spoonful of yogurt and some chopped fresh coriander or mint.

To microwave:

1. Put the oil, onion, garlic, ginger and curry paste into a large casserole. Cook on HIGH for about 3 minutes until soft.

2. Add the parsnips, potatoes and the *hot* stock. Cover and cook on HIGH for about 12 minutes, stirring once or twice, or until the parsnips are very soft.

3. As steps 3-6 above.

To freeze:
Cool and freeze at the end of step 5.

TIP:

Instead of milk or cream, add a spoonful or two of dried skimmed milk to a soup. It adds creaminess without the extra liquid and fat.

Cream of Celery and Bacon

A delicious soup for a winter's day! I prefer the flavour of this soup when it is made with chicken stock. You can of course use vegetable stock instead.

Serves 4

40g/1½ oz butter
1 medium onion, finely chopped
1 plump garlic clove, crushed
1 celery head, trimmed, separated and thickly sliced
225g/8 oz lean back bacon rashers
850ml/1½ pt chicken or vegetable stock
1 tsp dried thyme, or 1 tbsp fresh leaves
salt and freshly milled pepper
3 tbsp dried skimmed milk
1 tsp oil

1. Melt the butter in a pan and add the onion, garlic and celery. Cook gently for about 15 minutes, stirring occasionally, until the vegetables are soft but not brown.

2. Reserve 4 bacon rashers and finely chop the remainder. Add the chopped bacon to the pan and cook for about 5 minutes, stirring occasionally.

3. Add the stock and thyme. Bring to the boil, cover and simmer gently for about 15 minutes or until the celery is very soft.

4. Leave to cool slightly, then tip the mixture into a food processor or liquidiser and purée until smooth. Season to taste, add the dried milk and purée again.

5. Cut the remaining bacon into thin strips . Heat the oil in a small non-stick pan and cook the bacon, stirring frequently, until crisp and brown.

6. Reheat the soup gently and serve topped with the crisp bacon pieces.

To microwave:

1. Put the butter, onion, garlic and celery into a large casserole. Cover and cook on HIGH for about 10 minutes, stirring occasionally, until the vegetables are soft.

2. Reserve 4 bacon rashers and finely chop the remainder. Stir the chopped bacon into the casserole, cover and cook on HIGH for 3 minutes.

3. Add half the *hot* stock and the thyme. Cover and cook on HIGH for about 10 minutes or until the celery is very soft.

4. Add the remaining stock, then continue as step 4 above.

5. As steps 5 and 6 above.

To freeze:

Cool and freeze at the end of step 4. Thaw and continue with steps 5 and 6.

Grilled Red Pepper Soup

Grilling the peppers first gives the soup a lovely smoky flavour.

Serves 6

3 large red peppers
1 tbsp olive oil
1 medium red onion, finely chopped
2 garlic cloves, finely chopped
1 tbsp sugar
400g can chopped tomatoes
1 litre/1¾ pt chicken or vegetable stock
4 tbsp torn fresh basil
salt and freshly milled pepper

To serve:
crème fraîche
basil leaves

1. Put the whole peppers under a preheated grill, 7-10cm/3-4 inches away from the heat. Grill them, turning frequently, until their skins are black and blistered. Carefully put them into a plastic bag and leave to cool.

2. Peel the skins off the cooled peppers, cut them open and collect the juices. Remove and discard all seeds and white membrane, then cut the flesh into small pieces.

3. Put the oil, onion, garlic and sugar into a pan. Cook gently for about 5 minutes, stirring occasionally, until soft and beginning to turn golden brown. Add the tomatoes, peppers (with their reserved juices), stock and basil. Bring to the boil, then simmer gently for about 15 minutes.

4. Leave to cool slightly, then tip the mixture into a food processor or liquidiser and purée until smooth. Season to taste.

5. Reheat gently and serve topped with a spoonful of crème fraîche and a few basil leaves.

To microwave:

1. As step 1 above.

2. As step 2 above.

3. Put the oil, onion, garlic and sugar into a large casserole. Cover and cook on HIGH for about 3 minutes until soft. Add the tomatoes, peppers (with their reserved juices), basil and half the *hot* stock. Cover and cook on HIGH for about 5 minutes or until the mixture comes to the boil. Stir, then cook for a further 5 minutes.

4. Add the remaining stock, then continue as step 4 above.

5. As step 5 above.

To freeze:
Cool and freeze at the end of step 4.

Carrot and Leek, with a hint of Orange

This light soup is good served as a starter, before a meat dish. Top it with some dainty croûtons and a few fine slivers of orange peel (pour boiling water over the strips of peel and leave them to stand while you make the soup).

Serves 4-6

25g/1 oz butter
1 medium onion, finely chopped
3 small leeks, thinly sliced
3 medium carrots, thinly sliced
1 small main-crop potato, diced
600ml/1 pt chicken or vegetable stock
2 tsp ground coriander
1 medium orange
about 300ml/½ pt milk
salt and freshly milled pepper

1. Melt the butter in a pan and add the onion, leeks, carrots and potato. Cook gently for about 10 minutes, stirring occasionally, until soft but not brown.

2. Add the stock and coriander. Finely grate 2 tsp of peel from the orange and add to the pot. Squeeze the juice from the orange and add it too.

3. Bring to the boil, cover, then simmer gently for about 10 minutes or until the vegetables are very soft.

4. Leave to cool slightly, then tip into a food processor or liquidiser and purée until smooth. Pour in the milk and purée again, adding a little extra if necessary to produce the required consistency. Season to taste.

5. Reheat and serve.

To microwave:

1. Put the butter, onion, leeks, carrots and potato into a large casserole. Cook on HIGH for about 5 minutes, stirring once or twice, until soft.

2. Add the *hot* stock and the coriander. Finely grate 2 tsp of peel from the orange and add to the casserole. Squeeze the juice from the orange and add it too.

3. Cover and cook on HIGH for about 10 minutes or until the vegetables are very soft.

4. Continue as steps 4-5 above.

To freeze:
Cool and freeze at the end of step 4.

Sweet Potato and Leek Soup

Sweet potato is often used in West Indian recipes. Here, it is made into a thick winter-warming soup.

Serves 4-6

25g/1 oz butter
1 tbsp oil
1 medium onion, finely chopped
550g/1¼ lb leeks, thinly sliced
550g/1¼ lb sweet potatoes, cut into 1cm/½ in dice
1 litre/1¾ pt chicken or vegetable stock, plus extra if necessary
salt and freshly milled pepper
chopped parsley and/or chives, to serve

1. Heat the butter and oil in a pan and add the onion and leeks. Cook gently for about 10 minutes, stirring occasionally, until soft but not brown.

2. Stir in the sweet potatoes and cook for about 5 minutes, stirring occasionally.

3. Add the stock. Bring to the boil, then simmer gently for about 20 minutes until the vegetables are very soft.

4. Leave to cool slightly, then tip into a food processor or liquidiser and purée until smooth (add a little extra stock if necessary to make a thick pouring consistency).

5. Season to taste, reheat and serve sprinkled with parsley and/or chives.

To microwave:
1. Put the butter, oil, onion and leeks into a large casserole. Cover and cook on HIGH for 5 minutes, stirring once, until soft.

2. Stir in the sweet potatoes and cook on HIGH for 5 minutes, stirring once.

3. Add half the *hot* stock. Cook on HIGH for 10-15 minutes or until the vegetables are very soft.

4. Add the remaining stock and continue as steps 4 and 5 above.

To freeze:
Cool and freeze at the end of step 4.

TIP:

When peeled, some varieties of sweet potatoes quickly turn black, so prepare them just before they are needed. Alternatively, immerse the pieces in acidulated water (add some lemon juice or vinegar) until required.

Spiced Courgette Soup

This is lovely served hot or chilled. Garnish it with some thin slices of courgette, either blanched or lightly fried in butter.

Serves 4

25g/1 oz butter
1 medium onion, finely chopped
1 plump garlic clove, crushed
1 tsp ground cumin
1 tsp ground coriander
350g/12 oz courgettes, sliced
140g/5 oz main-crop potato, sliced
425ml/¾ pt chicken or vegetable stock
300ml/½ pt milk
salt and freshly milled pepper

1. Melt the butter in a pan and add the onion and garlic. Cook gently for about 5 minutes, stirring occasionally, until soft but not brown.

2. Add the cumin and coriander and cook, stirring for 2 minutes.

3. Add the courgettes, potato, stock and milk. Bring to the boil, then cover and simmer gently for about 15 minutes until the vegetables are soft.

4. Leave to cool slightly, then tip into a food processor or liquidiser and purée until smooth.

5. Season to taste and reheat if necessary.

To microwave:

1. Put the butter, onion and garlic into a large casserole. Cover and cook on HIGH for about 3 minutes or until soft.

2. Add the cumin and coriander and cook on HIGH for 1 minute.

3. Add the courgettes, potatoes and *hot* stock. Cover and cook on HIGH for about 10 minutes, stirring once, or until the vegetables are soft.

4. Stir in the milk, then continue as steps 4 and 5 above.

To freeze:
Cool and freeze at the end of step 5.

Creamy Potato Soup with Nutmeg

Nutmeg complements potatoes to give a wonderful flavour to this soup. Use freshly grated nutmeg if you can.

Serves 4-6

25g/1 oz butter
1 medium onion, thinly sliced
1 plump garlic clove
550g/1¼ lb main-crop potatoes, sliced
700ml/1¼ pt light vegetable stock
salt and freshly milled pepper
300ml/½ pt milk
¼ tsp grated nutmeg
3 tbsp double cream
chopped fresh parsley, to garnish

1. Melt the butter in a pan and add the onion, garlic and potatoes. Cook gently for about 10 minutes, stirring occasionally, without browning.

2. Add the stock and seasoning. Bring to the boil, cover and simmer gently for about 25 minutes until the vegetables are very soft.

3. Leave to cool slightly, then tip into a food processor or liquidiser and purée until smooth.

4. Return the soup to the pan and stir in the milk and nutmeg. Bring to the boil, then simmer gently for 5 minutes.

5. Stir in the cream and serve, sprinkled with parsley.

To microwave:

1. Put the butter, onion, potatoes and garlic into a large casserole. Cover and cook on HIGH for 5 minutes, stirring once.

2. Add half the *hot* stock and seasoning. Cover and cook on HIGH for about 15 minutes, stirring once or twice, until the vegetables are very soft.

3. Add the remaining stock then continue as step 3 above.

4. Return the soup to the casserole and stir in the milk and nutmeg. Cook on HIGH for 5 minutes, stirring once.

5. As step 5 above.

To freeze:
Cool and freeze after adding the milk and nutmeg in step 4. Thaw and reheat the soup, then continue with step 5.

Mushroom and Herb Soup

This soup seems to be a favourite with adults and children alike. For a dark, well-flavoured soup, use flat open mushrooms; for a light, delicate soup, use button or closed-cup mushrooms. I like to use open-cup brown-cap mushrooms.

Serves 4-6

40g/1½ oz butter
2 medium onions, finely chopped
225g/8 oz mushrooms, thinly sliced
25g/1 oz flour
850ml/1½ pt vegetable or chicken stock
300ml/½ pt milk
3 tbsp chopped fresh herbs, such as parsley or coriander, plus
    extra for garnish
salt and freshly milled pepper
1 tbsp lemon juice
3 tbsp double cream (optional)

1. Melt the butter in a pan and add the onions. Cook gently for about 5 minutes, stirring occasionally, until soft but not brown.

2. Stir in the mushrooms, then the flour. Gradually stir in the stock. Add the milk and herbs. Bring to the boil, stirring, then cover and simmer gently for 10 minutes.

3. Leave to cool slightly, then tip the mixture into a food processor or liquidiser and purée until smooth. Season to taste.

4. Remove from the heat, stir in the lemon juice and cream. Serve, garnished with extra herbs.

To microwave:

1. Put the butter and onions in a large casserole. Cover and cook on HIGH for about 5 minutes, stirring once, until soft.

2. Stir in the mushrooms, then the flour. Gradually stir in half the *hot* stock and herbs. Cover and cook on HIGH for 10 minutes. Add the remaining stock and the milk.

3. Continue as step 3 above.

4. As step 4 above.

To freeze:

Cool and freeze at the end of step 3. Thaw and reheat the soup, then continue with step 4.

Fennel and Apple Soup

Another soup which is good served hot or chilled. If you want a really smooth finish, pass it through a fine nylon sieve at the end of step 3.

Serves 4-6

2 medium fennel bulbs
25g/1 oz butter
1 medium onion, finely chopped
3 eating apples, peeled, cored and chopped
1 litre/1¾ pt vegetable or chicken stock
salt and freshly milled pepper
soured cream or thick Greek-style yogurt

1. Trim and thinly slice the fennel, reserving a few of the green fronds for garnish.

2. Melt the butter in a pan and add the onion. Cook gently for about 5 minutes, stirring occasionally, until soft but not brown. Stir in the fennel and apples and cook, stirring, for 1-2 minutes.

3. Add the stock, bring to the boil, then simmer gently for 20-30 minutes until the fennel is very soft.

4. Leave to cool slightly, then tip into a food processor or liquidiser and purée until smooth. Season to taste.

5. Ladle into bowls and serve topped with a spoonful of cream or yogurt. Snip the reserved fennel fronds on top.

To microwave:
1. As step 1 above.

2. Put the butter and onion into a casserole, cover and cook for 2 minutes. Stir in the fennel and apples, cover and cook for 3 minutes.

3. Add half the *hot* stock. Cover and cook on HIGH for about 15 minutes, stirring once, or until the fennel is very soft.

4. Add the remaining stock and continue with step 4 above.

5. As step 5 above.

To freeze:
Cool and freeze at the end of step 4.

Butterbean Soup with Chorizo

Chorizo is a spicy Spanish sausage. If none is available, use smoked sausage or frankfurters instead.

Serves 4-6

25g/1 oz butter
1 medium onion, finely chopped
1 plump garlic clove, crushed
1 medium carrot, thinly sliced
1 celery stick, thinly sliced
1 medium main-crop potato, sliced
420g can butterbeans
1 litre/1¾ pt chicken or vegetable stock
salt and freshly milled pepper
1 tbsp olive oil
about 115g/4 oz chorizo sausage, thinly sliced

1. Melt the butter in a pan and add the onion. Cook over medium heat for about 5 minutes, stirring occasionally, or until the onion is soft and golden brown.

2. Stir in the garlic, carrot, celery and potato. Add the beans (including their juice), stock and seasoning. Bring to the boil, cover and simmer gently for about 15 minutes or until the vegetables are very soft.

3. Leave to cool slightly, then tip into a food processor or liquidiser and purée until smooth. Return to the pan and adjust the seasoning to taste.

4. In a small frying pan, heat the oil and quickly cook the sausage, stirring until golden brown. Lift out and drain on absorbent kitchen paper.

5. Reheat the soup and serve with the sausage scattered over the top.

To microwave:

1. Put the butter and onion into a casserole, cover and cook on HIGH for about 3 minutes or until soft.

2. Stir in the garlic, carrot, celery and potato. Add the beans (including their juice), half the *hot* stock and the seasoning. Cover and cook on HIGH for about 10 minutes, stirring once or twice, or until the vegetables are very soft.

3. Add the remaining stock and continue as step 3 above.

4. As steps 4 and 5 above.

To freeze:

Cool and freeze at the end of step 3. Thaw, then continue with steps 4 and 5.

Creamy Onion and Rosemary

No rosemary? Use thyme instead to make a different, but delicious, soup.

Serves 4

25g/1 oz butter
450g/1 lb onions, thinly sliced
1 plump garlic clove, thinly sliced
1 tsp dried rosemary, or 1 tbsp fresh
700ml/1¼ pt vegetable stock
salt and freshly milled pepper
150ml/¼ pt double cream
50ml/2 fl oz dry sherry (optional)
snipped chives, to garnish

1. Melt the butter in a pan and add the onions, garlic and rosemary. Cook gently for about 10 minutes, stirring occasionally, until soft but not brown.

2. Stir in the stock, bring to the boil and simmer gently for about 15 minutes, until the onions are very soft.

3. Leave to cool slightly, then tip the mixture into a food processor or liquidiser and purée until smooth. Pass through a nylon sieve to remove any woody pieces of rosemary.

4. Season to taste and stir in the cream and sherry (if using). Reheat gently and serve, garnished with chives.

To microwave:
1. Put the butter, onions, garlic and rosemary into a large casserole. Cover and cook on HIGH for about 5 minutes, stirring once, or until the onions are very soft.

2. Stir in the stock, cover and cook on HIGH for 10 minutes.

3. Continue as steps 3-4 above.

To freeze:
Cool and freeze at the end of step 3. Reheat the soup and, just before serving, add the cream and sherry (if using).

Cream of Cauliflower and Broccoli

Though I like to use a mixture of cauliflower and broccoli, you could of course use just one.

Serves 4-6

25g/1 oz butter
1 large onion, thinly sliced
1 medium main-crop potato, thinly sliced
225g/8 oz cauliflower florets
225g/8 oz broccoli florets
600ml/1 pt vegetable stock
salt and freshly milled pepper
300ml/½ pt milk
4 tbsp double cream
grated cheese, to serve
chopped fresh parsley, to serve

1. Melt the butter in a pan and add the onion. Cook gently for about 5 minutes, stirring occasionally, or until soft but not brown.

2. Stir in the potato, cauliflower and broccoli. Add the stock and seasoning. Bring to the boil, cover and simmer gently for about 20 minutes until the vegetables are very soft.

3. Leave to cool slightly, then tip into a processor or liquidiser and purée until smooth.

4. Return the mixture to the pan and stir in the milk. Reheat, adjust seasoning to taste and stir in the cream.

5. Ladle into warm bowl and top with some grated cheese and chopped parsley.

To microwave:
1. Put the butter and onion into a casserole, cover and cook on HIGH for about 4 minutes, stirring once, until soft.

2. Stir in the potato, cauliflower and broccoli. Add the *hot* stock and seasoning. Cover and cook on HIGH for about 10 minutes, stirring once, or until the vegetables are very soft.

3. Continue as steps 3-5 above.

To freeze:
Cool and freeze at the end of step 4.

6

MAIN-MEAL SOUPS

The soups in this section are filling and hearty – they are meant to be served just as they are. Each one is substantial enough to be served as a meal in itself. Choose them for a snack, for lunch or for supper and serve generous portions in large bowls with plenty of crusty bread.

Cullen Skink

This recipe is based on the smoked fish and potato soup traditionally served in Scotland.

Serves 4

450g/1 lb new potatoes, thinly sliced
450g/1 lb smoked haddock fillet
1 medium onion, finely chopped
600ml/1 pt vegetable stock
6 black peppercorns
300ml/½ pt milk
salt and freshly milled pepper
chopped fresh parsley

1. Cook the potatoes in boiling salted water until tender.
2. Meanwhile, arrange the fish in a shallow pan and add the onion, stock and peppercorns. Bring to the boil, then simmer very gently for about 10 minutes or until the fish is cooked.
3. Lift the fish from the pan, reserving the stock and onion and discarding the peppercorns. Flake the fish, discarding skin and bones.
4. Drain the potatoes and return them to the rinsed pan. Add the flaked fish and the reserved stock and onion. Stir in the milk then season to taste.
5. Heat gently until hot. Serve sprinkled with parsley.

To microwave:
1. Arrange the fish in a shallow dish. Add three-quarters of the *hot* stock, the onion and peppercorns. Cover and cook for 5 minutes. Leave to stand covered.
2. Meanwhile, put the potatoes into a large casserole with the remaining stock. Cover and cook on HIGH for 8-10 minutes, stirring once or twice, until tender.
3. Lift the fish from the dish, reserving the stock and onion and discarding the peppercorns. Flake the fish, discarding skin and bones.
4. Add the fish to the potatoes in the casserole. Stir in the reserved stock and onion. Add the milk and season to taste.
5. As step 5 above.

Not suitable for freezing.

Mulligatawny Soup

This is my version of the Anglo-Indian dish. Use mild, medium or hot curry powder, according to your taste. Naan bread is the ideal accompaniment here.

Serves 4

40g/1½ oz butter
1 large onion, thinly sliced
1 small carrot, finely chopped
2 small celery sticks, thinly sliced
1 plump garlic clove, finely chopped
25g/1 oz flour
2 tsp curry powder
1.2 litre/2 pt chicken stock
1 large cooking apple
2 tsp lemon juice
25g/1 oz basmati rice
25-55g/1-2 oz cooked chicken meat, cut into shreds
salt and freshly milled pepper
4 tbsp single cream
2 tbsp fresh coriander leaves, roughly chopped

1. Melt the butter in a pan and stir in the onion, carrot, celery and garlic. Cook gently for about 10 minutes, stirring occasionally, until soft but not brown.

2. Stir in the flour and curry powder. Cook, stirring, for 2-3 minutes. Gradually blend in the stock and cook, stirring, until the mixture comes to the boil and thickens slightly. Cover and simmer gently for 30 minutes, stirring occasionally.

3. Peel, core and dice the apple and add to the pan with the lemon juice, rice and chicken. Season with salt and pepper.

4. Cover and simmer gently for about 15 minutes, or until the rice is tender.

5. Stir in the cream and coriander and serve.

To microwave:

1. Put the butter, onion, carrot, celery and garlic into a large casserole. Cover and cook on HIGH for about 5 minutes, stirring once or twice, until soft.

2. Stir in the flour and curry powder and cook, uncovered, for 2 minutes. Gradually blend in half the *hot* stock. Cook on HIGH for about 5 minutes, stirring once or twice, until the mixture comes to the boil and thickens. Cover and cook on MEDIUM for 10 minutes.

3. As step 3 above.

4. Add the remaining *hot* stock. Cover and cook on HIGH for about 10 minutes or until the rice is tender.

5. Stir in the cream and coriander and serve.

Not suitable for freezing.

Lentil and Bacon Soup

Serve this with a generous hunk of crusty bread. I like to top the soup with a swirl of double cream or some grated cheese.

Serves 6

1 tbsp oil
115g/4 oz lean streaky bacon, rinds removed and chopped
1 large onion, finely chopped
2 medium carrots, finely chopped
225g/8 oz red lentils
1.5 litre/2¾ pt ham, chicken or vegetable stock
2 tbsp tomato purée
salt and freshly milled pepper

1. Heat the oil in a pan and cook the bacon, stirring occasionally until it just begins to brown.

2. Stir in the onion and carrots and cook gently for about 5 minutes, stirring occasionally, until the onions are pale golden brown.

3. Stir in the lentils, stock and tomato purée. Bring to the boil, cover and simmer gently for about 30 minutes until the lentils and vegetables are very soft.

4. Leave to cool slightly, then tip into a food processor or liquidiser and purée until smooth.

5. Season to taste, reheat and serve.

To microwave:

1. Put the oil and bacon into a large casserole. Cook on HIGH for 3 minutes, stirring once.

2. Add the onion and carrots. Cover and cook on HIGH for about 5 minutes, stirring once, until the onions are very soft.

3. Stir in the lentils, half the *hot* stock and tomato purée. Cook on HIGH for about 5 minutes or until the mixture comes to the boil, then cover and cook on MED-LOW for about 30 minutes until the lentils and vegetables are very soft.

4. Add the remaining stock, then continue as step 4 above.

5. As step 5 above.

To freeze:
Cool and freeze at the end of step 4.

Minestrone

This recipe was originally developed as a quick microwave soup, but it works just as well on the hob. If you like, make it more substantial by adding a drained can of haricot beans. Sometimes, I like to add a finely chopped rasher of bacon with the vegetables in step 1.

Serves 4

1 tbsp olive oil
1 small onion, finely chopped
1 plump garlic clove, thinly sliced
2 medium carrots, cut into small dice
2 small celery sticks, thinly sliced
850ml/1½ pt vegetable stock
3 sun-dried tomatoes, finely chopped
50g/1¾ oz frozen peas
50g/1¾ oz small pasta shapes
50g/1¾ oz cabbage, finely shredded
2 tbsp chopped fresh parsley
salt and freshly milled pepper

To serve:
freshly grated or shaved Parmesan cheese

1. Put the oil, onion, garlic, carrots and celery into a pan and cook gently for about 5 minutes, stirring occasionally, until slightly soft but not brown.

2. Add the stock and bring to the boil. Cover and simmer gently for about 10 minutes.

3. Stir in the tomatoes, peas and pasta. Simmer gently for 8-10 minutes, stirring once or twice, until the pasta is just tender.

4. Stir in the cabbage and parsley, remove from the heat and leave to stand for 2-3 minutes. Season to taste.

5. Serve, sprinkled with Parmesan cheese.

To microwave:

1. Put the oil, onion, garlic, carrots and celery into a large casserole. Stir in half the *hot* stock. Cover and cook on HIGH for about 5 minutes, stirring once or twice, until the vegetables are just tender.

2. Stir in the tomatoes, peas, pasta and remaining stock. Cook on HIGH for about 5 minutes, stirring occasionally, or until the soup comes to the boil.

3. Stir in the cabbage and parsley. Cook on HIGH for 2-3 minutes. Season to taste.

4. Serve, sprinkled with Parmesan cheese.

Not suitable for freezing.

Scotch Broth with Lamb

A modern version of a traditional winter-warming dish. I have cut about an hour off the original cooking time. This recipe takes a similar time to cook, whether on the hob or in the microwave.

Serves 6

1 tbsp oil
6 lean best-end-of-neck lamb cutlets, trimmed of excess fat
1.5 litre/2¾ pt lamb stock
3 tbsp pearl barley
4 tbsp dried green peas, soaked in cold water overnight and
   drained
1 large onion, finely chopped
1 large carrot, cut into small dice
about 175g/6 oz swede, cut into small dice
salt and freshly milled pepper
about 175g/6 oz cabbage, shredded
2 medium leeks, thinly sliced
4 tbsp chopped fresh parsley

1. Heat the oil in a large pan and quickly brown the lamb on all sides.

2. Add the stock, barley and peas. Bring to the boil, cover and simmer gently for 30 minutes.

3. Add the onion, carrot, swede and seasoning. Bring to the boil, cover and simmer gently for another 30 minutes or until the barley and vegetables are soft.

4. Stir in the cabbage and leeks. Bring to the boil, then cover and simmer gently for a final 10-15 minutes.

5. Stir in the parsley. Serve each person with a lamb chop, some vegetables and plenty of the broth.

To microwave:

1. As step 1 above.

2. Transfer the lamb to a large casserole and add half the *hot* stock, barley, and peas. Cook on HIGH for about 5 minutes or until just boiling. Cover and cook on MEDIUM for 20 minutes.

3. Add the onion, carrot, swede and seasoning. Cook on HIGH for about 5 minutes or until the mixture comes to the boil. Cover and cook on MEDIUM for 30 minutes or until the barley and vegetables are soft.

4. Stir in the cabbage and leeks. Cook on HIGH for about 5 minutes or until boiling. Cover and cook on MEDIUM for 10 minutes.

5. As above.

Not suitable for freezing.

Chilli Beef and Red Bean Soup

A robust soup which needs only some good fresh bread to accompany it. Adjust the amount of chilli sauce to suit your own taste.

Serves 4

1 tbsp oil
1 large onion, finely chopped
1 plump garlic clove, finely chopped
1 tsp sugar
225g/8 oz frying steak, thinly sliced
400g can chopped tomatoes
700ml/1¼ pt beef stock (see TIP)
2 tbsp chopped fresh herbs or 1 tbsp dried mixed herbs
about 1 tsp chilli sauce
400g can red kidney beans, drained
salt and freshly milled pepper

1. Heat the oil in a pan and add the onion, garlic and sugar. Cook gently for about 10 minutes, stirring occasionally, until soft and golden brown.

2. Stir in the steak and cook for about 5 minutes, stirring occasionally, until brown.

3. Add the tomatoes, stock, herbs, chilli sauce and beans. Bring to the boil, then cover and simmer gently for about 20 minutes, or until the steak is tender.

4. Season to taste.

To microwave:

1. Put the oil, onion, garlic and sugar into a large casserole. Cover and cook on HIGH for about 5 minutes, stirring once, or until soft.

2. Stir in the steak and cook for 3 minutes, stirring once.

3. Add the tomatoes, *hot* stock, herbs, chilli sauce and beans. Cover and cook on HIGH for about 10 minutes or until the mixture comes to the boil. Stir, cover and cook on MEDIUM for about 20 minutes or until the steak is tender.

4. Season to taste.

Not suitable for freezing.

TIP:

In place of beef stock, you could use a can of good-quality consommé, made up to 700ml/1¼ pt with water.

Celery and Stilton Soup

The traditional partnership of celery with Stilton makes a filling soup with a rich flavour. I like to purée most of the soup, leaving some chunky bits. Serve with plenty of fresh crusty bread.

Serves 6

40g/1½ oz butter
1 medium onion, finely chopped
1 medium main-crop potato, chopped
1 celery head, thinly sliced
850ml/1½ pt chicken or vegetable stock
salt and freshly milled pepper
85g/3 oz Stilton cheese
150ml/¼ pt single cream

1. Melt the butter in a large pan and cook the onion gently for about 5 minutes, stirring occasionally, until soft but not brown.

2. Stir in the potato and celery. Cook over medium heat for 5 minutes, stirring occasionally, without browning.

3. Add the stock and season with pepper. Bring to the boil, cover and simmer gently for about 30 minutes or until the vegetables are very soft.

4. Leave to cool slightly then tip three-quarters of the mixture into a food processor or liquidiser. Purée until smooth.

5. Return the purée to the pan and stir well. Reheat and adjust the seasoning if necessary.

6. Remove from the heat, crumble in half the cheese and stir in the cream. Once the cheese has melted into the soup, serve, crumbling a little of the remaining cheese on top of each bowl.

To microwave:

1. Put the butter and onion into a large casserole and cook on HIGH for about 3 minutes, stirring once, until soft.

2. Stir in the potato and celery. Cover and cook on HIGH for 5 minutes, stirring once.

3. Add half the *hot* stock and season with pepper. Cover and cook on HIGH for about 15 minutes or until the vegetables are very soft.

4. Add the remaining stock and continue as step 4 above.

5. As step 5 above.

6. As step 6 above.

To freeze:
Cool and freeze at the end of step 5. Thaw, reheat and complete step 6.

Vegetable Soup with Cheddar and Mustard

Ideal for serving on a chilly day, this recipe is compiled from store-cupboard ingredients.

Serves 4

2 medium onions, finely chopped
4 medium carrots, thinly sliced
2 medium celery sticks, thinly sliced
425ml/¾ pt vegetable stock
300ml/½ pt milk
25g/1 oz flour
1 tbsp ready-made mustard, such as Dijon or wholegrain
115g/4 oz Cheddar cheese, grated
salt and freshly milled pepper

1. Put the vegetables and stock into a pan and bring to the boil. Cover and simmer gently for about 25 minutes, or until the vegetables are very tender.

2. Gradually blend the milk into the flour until smooth, then stir into the pan. Cook, stirring, until the soup comes to the boil.

3. Simmer gently for 5 minutes. Stir in the mustard.

4. Remove the pan from the heat and add half the cheese. Stir until it has melted. Season to taste.

5. Ladle into warm bowls and serve sprinkled with the remaining cheese.

To microwave:
1. Put the vegetables into a large casserole and add half the *hot* vegetable stock. Cover and cook on HIGH for about 10 minutes, stirring occasionally, or until the vegetables are very tender.

2. Gradually blend the milk into the flour, then stir into the casserole. Cook on HIGH for about 5 minutes, stirring occasionally, or until the soup comes to the boil.

3. Cover and cook on MEDIUM for 5 minutes. Stir in the mustard.

4. Add the remaining *hot* stock, then continue as steps 4 and 5 above.

Not suitable for freezing.

Butternut Squash and Coriander Soup

Butternut squash has brilliant orange flesh which gives this soup its beautiful colour. Serve it with croûtons.

Serves 4

550g/1¼ lb butternut squash
40g/1½ oz butter
1 medium onion, thinly sliced
225g/8 oz main-crop potatoes, thinly sliced
700ml/1¼ pt chicken or vegetable stock
150ml/¼ pt double cream
salt and freshly milled pepper
4 tbsp chopped fresh coriander

1. Cut the squash into quarters and scoop out and discard the seeds. Peel and slice the flesh.

2. Melt the butter in a pan and add the onion. Cook gently for about 5 minutes, stirring occasionally, until soft but not brown.

3. Stir in the squash and potatoes and cook, stirring, for 2-3 minutes. Add the stock. Bring to the boil, then cover and simmer gently for about 20 minutes or until the squash is very soft.

4. Leave to cool slightly, then tip into a food processor or liquidiser and purée until smooth. Add the cream and purée again. Season to taste.

5. Reheat gently, stir in the coriander and serve.

To microwave:
1. As step 1 above.

2. Put the butter and onion into a large casserole. Cover and cook on HIGH for 3 minutes or until soft.

3. Stir in the squash, potato and half the *hot* stock. Cover and cook on HIGH for about 15 minutes, stirring once or twice, or until the vegetables are very soft.

4. Add the remaining stock, then continue as step 4 above.

5. As step 5 above.

To freeze:
Cool and freeze at the end of step 4.

Chicken Chowder

I like to use new potatoes in this recipe. Alternatively, use a main-crop variety which will hold its shape, such as Estima, Cara or Desirée. Serve it with crusty rolls.

Serves 4-6

25g/1 oz butter
1 medium onion, finely chopped
4 celery sticks, thinly sliced
225g/8 oz potatoes (preferably new)
1 large boneless chicken breast, skinned and cut into small
  cubes
4 boneless chicken thighs, skinned and cut into small cubes
600ml/1 pt chicken stock
600ml/1 pt milk
175g/6 oz frozen (or drained canned) sweetcorn
salt and freshly milled pepper

1. Melt the butter in a pan and stir in the onion, celery and potatoes. Cook gently for about 5 minutes, stirring occasionally, until soft but not brown. Add the chicken and cook, stirring, for a few minutes until the chicken is no longer pink.

2. Stir in the stock. Bring to the boil, cover and simmer gently for about 15 minutes, stirring once or twice, or until the chicken and potatoes are tender but still hold their shape.

3. Add the milk, sweetcorn and seasoning to taste. Heat gently to serving temperature.

To microwave:

1. Put the butter, onion, celery and potatoes into a large casserole. Cover and cook on HIGH for about 5 minutes, stirring once, until soft.

2. Stir in the chicken, then add the hot stock. Cover and cook on HIGH for about 5 minutes, or until the mixture comes to the boil. Continue cooking on MEDIUM for 5-10 minutes, stirring once or twice, until the chicken and potatoes are tender but still hold their shape.

3. Add the milk, sweetcorn and seasoning to taste. Heat on HIGH for about 2 minutes or until serving temperature.

Not suitable for freezing.

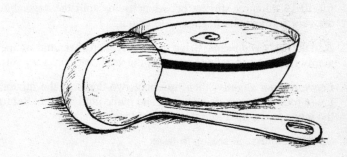

Fennel and Bean Soup

Fennel has a wonderful aniseed flavour, while the beans add substance to the soup.

Serves 4-6

2 tbsp olive oil
1 medium onion, finely chopped
1 medium leek, thinly sliced
2 plump garlic cloves, crushed
1 plump fennel bulb, thinly sliced
850ml/1½ pt chicken or vegetable stock
400g can cannellini or haricot beans, drained
300ml/½ pt milk
salt and freshly milled pepper

To serve:
freshly shaved Parmesan cheese
chopped chives
lemon wedges

1. Put the oil, onion, leek, garlic and fennel into a pan. Cook gently for 10-15 minutes, stirring occasionally, or until the vegetables are very soft and just beginning to colour.

2. Add the stock and beans. Bring to the boil, then cover and simmer gently for about 15 minutes or until the vegetables are very soft.

3. Leave to cool slightly, then tip about two-thirds of the mixture into a food processor or liquidiser and purée until smooth. Return the purée to the mixture remaining in the pan.

4. Stir in the milk and season to taste.

5. Reheat and serve topped with Parmesan shavings and chives. Let each person squeeze a lemon wedge over their serving, adding juice to taste.

To microwave:

1. Put the oil, onion, leek, garlic and fennel into a large casserole. Cover and cook on HIGH for about 7 minutes, stirring occasionally, or until the vegetables are very soft.

2. Add half the *hot* stock and the beans. Cover and cook on HIGH for about 5 minutes, then on MEDIUM for about 10 minutes, stirring once.

3. Add the remaining stock and continue as steps 3-5 above.

To freeze:
Cool and freeze at the end of step 4.

Sweetcorn and Tuna Chowder

Turn some frozen sweetcorn and a small can of tuna into a delicious stew-like soup.

Serves 4

40g/1½ oz butter
1 medium onion, thinly sliced
1 medium carrot, finely chopped
2 celery sticks, thinly sliced
3 tbsp plain flour
600ml/1 pt milk
600ml/1 pt hot vegetable stock
1 red pepper, seeds removed and chopped
225g/8 oz frozen sweetcorn kernels
finely grated rind and juice of 1 lemon
200g can tuna in brine, drained and flaked
salt and freshly milled pepper
100g/3½ oz mature Cheddar cheese, grated

1. Melt the butter in a pan and stir in the onion, carrot and celery. Cook gently for about 10 minutes, stirring occasionally, or until soft but not brown.

2. Stir in the flour and cook for 1-2 minutes. Gradually stir in the milk then cook, stirring continuously, until the mixture boils and thickens.

3. Stir in the stock, pepper and sweetcorn. Cover and simmer gently for 10-15 minutes until the vegetables are tender.

4. Add the lemon rind and juice and the drained tuna. Season to taste.

5. Reheat gently and serve, topping each bowl of soup with some cheese.

To microwave:

1. Put the butter, onion, carrot and celery into a large casserole. Cover and cook on HIGH for about 5 minutes, stirring once or twice, until soft.

2. Stir in the flour, then gradually stir in the milk. Cook on HIGH for about 5 minutes, stirring occasionally, or until the mixture comes to the boil and thickens.

3. Stir in the stock, pepper and sweetcorn. Cover and cook on HIGH for about 10 minutes, stirring once, or until the vegetables are tender.

4. As steps 4 and 5 above.

Not suitable for freezing.

Cock-a-Leekie with Mini Dumplings

For a lighter soup to serve as a first course (in which case the recipe will serve 6) omit the dumplings and simply garnish with chopped fresh parsley.

Serves 4

350g/12 oz leeks
25g/1 oz butter
1 large chicken portion, such as leg
1 litre/1¾ pt chicken stock
1 bouquet garni
salt and freshly milled black pepper
8 ready-to-eat dried prunes, each cut into 4 slivers

Dumplings:
100g/3½ oz self-raising flour
pinch of salt
freshly milled black pepper
50g/1¾ oz suet
2 tbsp chopped fresh parsley

1. Thinly slice the white parts of the leeks, reserving the green parts.

2. Melt the butter in a large pan and brown the chicken on all sides. Add the white leeks and cook gently for about 5 minutes, stirring occasionally, until soft.

3. Add the stock and bouquet garni. Season with salt and pepper. Bring to the boil, then simmer gently for about 30 minutes or until the chicken is very tender.

4. Lift out the chicken and cut the meat into small pieces, discarding skin and bones.

5. Make the dumplings. Sift the flour with salt and some pepper. Stir in the suet. Add sufficient cold water to make a soft but manageable dough. With floured fingers, shape the dough into about 16 small balls.

6. Thinly slice the reserved green leeks and add to the pan with the prunes and chicken. Bring to the boil.

7. Drop the dumplings into the soup, cover and simmer gently for about 15 minutes until swollen and cooked.

To microwave:

1. As step 1 above.

2. Put the butter and white leeks into a large casserole, cover and cook on HIGH for about 3 minutes until soft.

3. Add the chicken, half the *hot* stock and the bouquet garni. Season with salt and pepper. Cover and cook on HIGH for about 5 minutes or until the mixture comes to the boil. Continue cooking on MEDIUM for about 15 minutes or until the chicken is very tender.

4. As step 4 above.

5. As step 5 above.

6. Thinly slice the reserved green leeks and add to the casserole with the prunes, chicken and remaining hot stock. Cover and cook for about 5 minutes or until the soup comes to the boil.

7. Drop the dumplings into the soup, cover and cook on MEDIUM for about 10 minutes or until swollen and cooked.

To freeze:
Omit the dumplings, cool and freeze at the end of step 6.

Haricot Bean Soup with Pasta, Parsley and Parmesan

Serve this with a selection of warmed Italian-style breads.

Serves 4

1 tbsp olive oil
1 small onion, finely chopped
1 plump garlic clove, crushed
1 small red pepper, seeds removed and diced
1 medium carrot, diced
1.2 litre/2 pt vegetable stock
400g can haricot beans, drained and rinsed
25g/1 oz small pasta shapes
salt and freshly milled pepper
4 tbsp finely chopped fresh parsley
4 tbsp freshly grated Parmesan cheese

1. Put the oil, onion and garlic into a pan and cook gently for about 5 minutes, stirring occasionally, until soft but not brown.

2. Add the pepper, carrot, and stock. Bring to the boil, then cover and simmer gently for 15-20 minutes.

3. Add the beans and pasta. Cover and cook gently for 8-10 minutes or until the pasta and vegetables are tender.

4. Season to taste and stir in the parsley. Serve piping hot, topped with the Parmesan cheese.

To microwave:
1. Put the oil, onion and garlic into a large casserole. Cover and cook on HIGH for 3 minutes until soft.

2. Add the pepper, carrots, and half the *hot* stock. Cover and cook on HIGH for 10 minutes, stirring once.

3. Add the beans and pasta. Cover and cook on HIGH for about 8 minutes or until the pasta and vegetables are tender.

4. Stir in the remaining stock and continue as step 4 above.

Not suitable for freezing.

Pasta Soup with Mediterranean Herbs

A fresh-tasting soup which is good served with freshly shaved Parmesan cheese and Hot Garlic Bread (page 24) or Bruschetta (page 26).

Serves 4-6

2 tbsp olive oil
1 medium onion, finely chopped
2 plump garlic cloves, finely chopped
2 lean streaky bacon rashers, finely chopped
1.2 litre/2 pt chicken stock
175g/6 oz dried pasta, such as shells
salt and freshly milled pepper
1 tbsp chopped fresh thyme leaves
1 tbsp chopped fresh oregano
4 ripe tomatoes, skinned, seeds removed and chopped
about 10 fresh basil leaves

1. Heat the oil in a pan and add the onion, garlic and bacon. Cook gently for about 10 minutes, stirring occasionally, until soft and beginning to brown.

2. Add the stock and bring to the boil.

3. Stir in the pasta, seasoning, thyme and oregano. Simmer gently for about 10 minutes until the pasta is soft.

4. Adjust the seasoning to taste and stir in the tomatoes. Tear the basil into shreds, add to the soup and serve.

To microwave:
1. Put the oil, onion, garlic and bacon into a large casserole. Cook on HIGH for about 5 minutes, stirring once, until soft.

2. Add the *hot* stock and cook on HIGH for about 5 minutes or until the mixture comes to the boil.

3. Stir in the pasta, seasoning, thyme and oregano. Cook, uncovered, on HIGH for about 10 minutes, stirring once or twice, or until the pasta is soft.

4. As step 4 above.

Not suitable for freezing.

French-Style Fish Soup

Choose your favourite types of fish, or whatever is available at the fishmonger's or supermarket. Serve the soup immediately it has cooked, ladled on to thick slices of toasted French bread.

Serves 4

25g/1 oz butter
1 large onion, finely chopped
2 plump garlic cloves, finely chopped or crushed
1 medium carrot, finely chopped
1 medium leek, thinly sliced
400g can chopped tomatoes
425ml/¾ pt fish stock
2 tsp mixed dried herbs
350g/¾ lb skinless fish fillets, cut into bite-size pieces
115g/4 oz peeled prawns
salt and freshly milled pepper
4 thick French bread slices

1. Melt the butter in a pan and add the onion, garlic, carrot and leek. Cook gently, for about 10 minutes, stirring occasionally, or until soft.

2. Add the tomatoes, stock and herbs. Bring to the boil, cover and simmer for 10 minutes.

3. Add the fish and simmer very gently for 5 minutes.

4. Add the prawns and simmer very gently for 2 minutes. Season to taste.

5. Toast the bread on both sides and place each piece in the base of a warmed bowl. Ladle the soup over the top and serve.

To microwave:

1. Put the butter into a large casserole and add the onion, garlic, carrot and leek. Cover and cook on HIGH for 5 minutes, stirring once or twice, until very soft.

2. Stir in the tomatoes, stock and herbs. Cover and cook on HIGH for about 5 minutes, or until the mixture comes to the boil. Cook on MEDIUM for 5 minutes.

3. Stir in the fish and cook on MEDIUM for 3 minutes.

4. Stir in the prawns and cook on MEDIUM for 2 minutes. Season to taste.

5. As step 5 above.

Not suitable for freezing.

Chinese Chicken and Vegetable Soup

A quick recipe which is just as good made with thinly sliced pork fillet in place of chicken. The juice from the ginger gives a warm delicate flavour.

Serves 4-6

1 tbsp oil
1 boneless chicken breast, skinned and thinly sliced
2 plump garlic cloves, crushed
1 small head of Chinese leaves, quartered lengthways and
   thickly sliced
85g/3 oz mushrooms, such as oyster
1 small red pepper, seeds removed and cut into small dice
55g/2 oz baby sweetcorn, thinly sliced
1 litre/1¾ pt chicken stock
3 tbsp soy sauce
85g/3 oz thread noodles
piece of fresh ginger, measuring about 5cm/2 in
4 spring onions, thinly sliced
salt and freshly milled pepper
2 tbsp chopped fresh coriander or parsley

1. Heat the oil in a pan or wok, add the chicken and cook quickly, stirring, until cooked and golden brown.

2. Stir in the garlic and cook, stirring, for 1 minute. Add the Chinese leaves, mushrooms, pepper and sweetcorn. Cook for 1-2 minutes, stirring.

3. Add the stock and soy sauce. Break the noodles into the pan.

4. Roughly grate the ginger and, scooping it up in your hand, squeeze hard so that the juice runs through your fingers and into the pan (discard the pulp).

5. Add the spring onions, bring to the boil, then simmer gently for 3-5 minutes until the noodles are soft.

6. Season to taste and stir in the coriander.

To microwave:

1. Put the oil into a large casserole and stir in the chicken and garlic. Cover and cook on HIGH for about 3 minutes, stirring once, or until the chicken is cooked through.

2. Add the Chinese leaves, mushrooms, pepper and sweetcorn. Cover and cook for 2 minutes.

3. Add the *hot* stock and soy sauce. Break the noodles into the casserole and stir well.

4. As step 4 above.

5. Add the spring onions, cover and cook on HIGH for about 8 minutes or until the mixture has come to the boil and the noodles are soft.

6. As step 6 above.

Not suitable for freezing.

TIP:

If, like me, you tend to lose pieces of fresh ginger root at the back of the fridge, only to shrivel up before they are used, keep a bottle of root ginger sauce handy instead. It makes an excellent alternative to ginger juice.

Leek and Potato Soup

This is probably the soup most often prepared in my family. Everyone seems to love it, particularly when it is served sprinkled with small pieces of crisp-cooked bacon or croûtons.

Serves 4-6

25g/1 oz butter
2 medium leeks, thinly sliced
1 medium onion, finely chopped
350g/12 oz main-crop potatoes, thinly sliced
700ml/1¼ pt chicken or vegetable stock
salt and freshly milled pepper
150ml/¼ pt milk
2-3 tbsp double cream
2 tbsp chopped fresh parsley

1. Melt the butter in a pan and add the leeks, onion and potatoes. Cook for about 10 minutes, stirring occasionally, until the vegetables begin to soften but not brown.
2. Add the stock and season with salt and pepper. Bring to the boil, then simmer gently for about 30 minutes until the vegetables are very soft.
3. Leave to cool slightly, then tip into a food processor or liquidiser and purée until smooth. Add the milk and purée again. Adjust seasoning to taste.
4. Reheat gently, stir in the cream and parsley and serve.

To microwave:

1. Put the butter, leeks, onion and potatoes into a large casserole. Cover and cook on HIGH for about 5 minutes, stirring once.
2. Add half the *hot* stock and season with salt and pepper. Cover and cook on HIGH for about 15 minutes, stirring occasionally, or until the vegetables are very soft.
3. Add the remaining stock, then continue as step 3 above.
4. As step 4 above.

To freeze:
Cool and freeze at the end of step 3.

TIP:
For a more chunky soup, in step 3, purée about two-thirds only, then stir it all together again.

7

SOUPS FOR DESSERT?

Why not? There is no rule which says that soups should be confined to savoury starters, snacks and meals. Serving soups at the 'wrong end of the meal' is guaranteed to stimulate conversation. The novelty of the idea will entertain your friends and family, ensuring fond memories of their visit to your place. Sweet fruit or chocolate mixtures are the best choices. Here are just a few recipes to try.

Chocolate and Vanilla Soup

This one is for chocolate lovers! Similar to a chocolate fondue, this dessert soup is at its most indulgent when you use a chocolate containing at least 50% cocoa solids. It's best served at room temperature.

Serves 4-6

125ml/4 fl oz milk
vanilla pod
225g/8 oz plain dark chocolate

To serve:
mixture of fresh fruits, cut into bite-size pieces
crisp biscuits, such as amaretti

1. Pour the milk into a non-stick pan. Split the vanilla pod to release the seeds. Add pod and seeds to the milk. Place the pan on a low heat and slowly bring the milk just to the boil. Remove from the heat and leave to stand for 5 minutes.

2. Meanwhile, break the chocolate into a bowl and place over a pan of simmering water, stirring occasionally, until melted.

3. Strain the milk and pour it over the chocolate. Gently whisk until smooth. Leave to cool to room temperature.

4. Warm some individual serving bowls. Spoon some fruit pieces into each bowl and pour the chocolate over the top. Serve with crisp biscuits for dipping.

To microwave:
1. Pour the milk into a bowl. Split the vanilla pod to release the seeds. Add pod and seeds to the milk. Heat the milk on MED-LOW for about 3 minutes or until the mixture comes just to the boil. Leave to stand for 5 minutes.

2. Meanwhile, break the chocolate into a bowl and heat on MED-LOW for about 10 minutes, stirring occasionally, until melted.

3. Continue as steps 3-4 above.

Not suitable for freezing.

Summer Fruit Soup

A refreshing and summery end to a meal.

Serves 4-6

675g/1½ lb summer fruit, such as raspberries or pitted cherries
3 tbsp lemon juice
2 tbsp caster sugar
150ml/¼ pt fruit juice, such as orange, pineapple or mango
300ml/½ pt sweet cider, plus extra if necessary
4 tbsp finely chopped fresh mint
mint leaves, for decoration

1. Put the fruit into a pan with the lemon juice and sugar. Heat gently, stirring, until the sugar dissolves, the fruit juices run and the mixture begins to bubble.

2. Remove from the heat and stir in the fruit juice.

3. Tip into a food processor or liquidiser and purée until smooth. Add the cider and purée again.

4. Pass the mixture through a fine nylon sieve. Stir in the mint.

5. Serve chilled, decorated with a mint leaf or two.

To microwave:
1. Put the fruit into a bowl with the lemon juice and sugar. Cook on HIGH, stirring occasionally, until the sugar dissolves, the fruit juices run and the mixture begins to bubble.

2. Continue as steps 2-5 above.

To freeze:
At the end of step 4.

Strawberry Soup with Whipped Cream

This is based on the wonderful, simple recipe created by the late Jane Grigson. In place of red wine, I have added the summery tipple, Pimms No.1.

Serves 4-6

675g/1½ lb ripe strawberries
1 tsp cornflour
about 75ml/2½ fl oz orange juice
about 85g/3 oz caster sugar
about 75ml/2½ fl oz Pimms No 1
whipped cream

1. Reserve 4-6 small whole strawberries for decoration. Blend the cornflour with the orange juice and set aside.

2. Thickly slice the remaining strawberries and put them into a pan with the sugar and 1 tbsp water. Heat gently, stirring occasionally, until the sugar dissolves, the juice runs from the strawberries and the mixture begins to bubble. Stir in the cornflour-and-orange mixture, then simmer very gently for about 10 minutes, stirring occasionally.

3. Leave to cool slightly, then tip into a processor or liquidiser and purée until smooth. Pass the mixture through a fine nylon sieve. Leave to cool.

4. Stir in the Pimms No 1. Taste, adjusting the sweetness and adding more Pimms according to taste.

5. Serve chilled, topped with a floating spoonful of whipped cream and the reserved strawberries.

To microwave:
1. As step 1 above.

2. Thickly slice the remainder and put them into a bowl with the sugar and 1 tbsp water. Cook on MED-HIGH for about 5 minutes, stirring occasionally, or until the sugar dissolves, the juice runs from the strawberries and the mixture begins to bubble. Stir in the cornflour-and-orange mixture, cover and cook on MED-LOW for about 10 minutes, stirring occasionally.

3. Continue with steps 3-5 above.

To freeze:
Freeze at the end of step 3. Thaw and continue with steps 4 and 5.

Melon and Ginger Soup

This is delicious as a light summer starter too.

Serves 4-6

115g/4 oz caster sugar
1 melon, yielding about 675g/1½ lb flesh
300ml/½ pt dry white wine
5cm/2 in piece of fresh root ginger
150ml/¼ pt crème fraîche, plus extra for serving

1. Put the sugar in a pan with 450ml/16 fl oz water. Heat gently until the sugar has dissolved and the mixture comes to the boil. Leave to cool.

2. Tip the melon into a food processor or liquidiser and add the wine. Purée until smooth.

3. Transfer to a bowl and stir in the sugar syrup. Roughly grate the ginger and, gathering it up in your hand, squeeze hard so that the juice runs through your fingers and into the bowl (discard the pulp). Whisk in the crème fraîche.

4. Serve chilled, with a swirl of crème fraîche on the top of each bowl.

To microwave:
1. Put the sugar in a bowl with 450m/16 fl oz water. Heat on HIGH, stirring occasionally, until the sugar dissolves and the mixture comes to the boil. Leave to cool.

2. Continue as steps 2-4 above.

Not suitable for freezing.

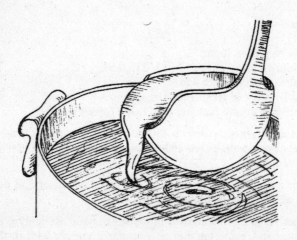

SAUCES

A good sauce can transform a rather ordinary meal into a memorable occasion. Whether its flavour is subtle or assertive, it can provide the "finishing touch" to the plate.

In the following sections, you will find sauces to complement all kinds of foods – from traditional recipes (brought up to date) to made-in-a-minute sauces using up-to-the-moment ingredients. To make the most of the limited number of pages, I have included those sauces which are most often made in my kitchen.

One little reminder: a lumpy sauce need not be the end of the world! Just tip it into a food processor or liquidiser and blend until smooth; alternatively, pass it through a fine sieve.

8

THICKENING SAUCES

There is sometimes a certain fear of sauce making. Don't pay any attention to it! Sauces need not be time consuming or complicated. To show you how simple it can be, here are the basic ways to thicken a flavoured liquid or sauce.

Reducing:
When the cooking juices are boiled or simmered, uncovered, until they bubble down to give a more concentrated mixture which is then served as a sauce. See Gravy, page 130.

Roux:
Equal quantities of butter and flour are cooked together before the liquid is added and the sauce is heated, stirring or whisking continuously, until it comes to the boil and thickens. The longer the butter-and-flour mixture is cooked, the darker the sauce. See Traditional White Sauce, page 121 and Espagnole Sauce, page 129.

Cornflour:
A good way to thicken a sauce in a hurry. Cornflour is blended with a little cold liquid to make a smooth paste, added to the sauce base and brought to the boil, stirring or whisking all the while. To thicken 300ml/½ pt sauce, use about 2 tsp cornflour blended with 2 tbsp cold liquid – water, stock, wine.

Arrowroot:
This is ideal for thickening clear liquids. Used in similar way to cornflour, it produces a less cloudy result.

Beurre manié:
Equal quantities of butter and flour are blended together, then added in small pieces to the bubbling sauce, until the sauce is sufficiently

thick. A good way of thickening pan juices to give a smooth glossy sauce. The butter-and-flour mixture can be kept in the fridge for a few weeks, ready for when you need it. See Mussel Soup with Coconut and Coriander, page 52.

Vegetable or fruit purée:
A simple sauce can be made from vegetables or fruit, cooked until they are very soft, then puréed. A thin sauce of this type is called a coulis.

Egg yolk and cream:
Can be used to thicken and enrich a sauce. This method needs extra care in order to prevent the mixture curdling. Mix an egg yolk with 1-2 tbsp cream and stir in a little of the hot sauce. Off the heat, whisk the mixture into the sauce. Cook gently, whisking continuously, until the sauce thickens – on no account letting it boil. (See TIP on page 132.)

9

TRADITIONAL SAVOURY SAUCES

Traditional White Sauce

This makes a sauce which is suitable for pouring. For a thicker sauce which will coat food, double the quantities of butter and flour.

Makes about 300ml/½ pt

15g/½ oz butter
15g/½ oz flour
300ml/½ pt milk
salt and freshly milled pepper

1. Melt the butter in a saucepan and stir in the flour. Cook gently for 1-2 minutes without allowing it to brown.

2. Remove the pan from the heat and gradually stir in the milk. Cook, stirring, until the sauce comes to the boil and thickens.

3. Simmer very gently for 2-3 minutes, stirring. Season to taste.

To microwave:
1. Put the butter in a bowl or jug and cook on HIGH for about 20 seconds or until melted. Stir in the flour. Cook on HIGH for 20 seconds.

2. Gradually stir in the milk. Cook on HIGH for about 3 minutes, stirring frequently, or until the sauce comes to the boil and thickens.

3. Season to taste.

To freeze:
Cool and freeze at the end of step 3.

One-Step White Sauce

Sometimes called an All-In-One sauce.

Makes about 300ml/¹/₂ pt.

Ingredients as for Traditional White Sauce

1. Put all the ingredients in a saucepan and heat, whisking continuously, until the sauce comes to the boil, thickens and is cooked.

To microwave:

1. Put the flour in a bowl or jug, gradually blend in the milk, then add the butter. Cook on HIGH for about 3 minutes, whisking frequently, until the sauce comes to the boil, thickens and is cooked.

To freeze:

Cool and freeze at the end of step 1.

Blended White Sauce

This version uses cornflour to make a pouring sauce. For a sauce which will coat food, use double the amount of cornflour. For a more savoury sauce, replace half the milk with stock.

Makes about 300ml/½ pt

1 tbsp cornflour
300ml/½ pt milk
knob of butter
salt and freshly milled pepper

1. Put the cornflour in a bowl and blend it with a little of the milk to make a smooth paste. Put the remaining milk and the butter into a saucepan and bring just to the boil. Pour on to the cornflour mixture, stirring continuously.

2. Transfer the mixture to the pan and cook, stirring, until the sauce comes to the boil and thickens.

3. Cook very gently for 2-3 minutes, stirring. Season to taste.

To microwave:
1. Put the cornflour in a bowl or jug and blend with a little of the milk to make a smooth paste. Stir in the remaining milk and add the butter.

2. Cook on MEDIUM for about 3 minutes, whisking frequently, or until the sauce comes to the boil, thickens and is cooked.

3. Season to taste.

To freeze:
Cool and freeze at the end of step 3.

Béchamel Sauce

A classic French coating sauce, used as the flavourful base of many other sauces. Serve this version with vegetable, egg, fish or poultry dishes. For a really velvety sauce and for special occasions, I like to add a little cream.

Makes about 300ml/½ pt

300ml/½ pt milk
1 shallot or very small onion, quartered
1 small carrot, thinly sliced
1 small celery stick, sliced
1 bay leaf
6-8 black peppercorns
pinch of grated nutmeg
25g/1 oz butter
25g/1 oz flour
salt and freshly milled pepper
2 tbsp single cream (optional)

1. Put the milk into a saucepan and add the shallot, carrot, celery, bay leaf, peppercorns and nutmeg. Heat slowly until the milk just comes to the boil. Remove from the heat, cover and leave to stand for 20-30 minutes for the flavours to infuse into the milk, then strain, reserving the milk.

2. Melt the butter in a clean saucepan and add the flour. Cook gently, stirring for 1-2 minutes without allowing it to brown.

3. Remove the pan from the heat and gradually stir in the flavoured milk. Cook, stirring, until the sauce comes to the boil and thickens.

4. Simmer very gently for 2-3 minutes, stirring. Season to taste and, if using, stir in the cream.

To microwave:

1. Put the milk into a bowl and add the shallot, carrot, celery, bay leaf, peppercorns and nutmeg. Heat on MEDIUM for about 5 minutes or until the milk just comes to the boil. Cover and leave to stand for 20-30 minutes for the flavours to infuse into the milk, then strain, reserving the milk.

2. Put the butter in a bowl or jug and cook on HIGH for about 20 seconds or until melted. Stir in the flour. Cook on HIGH for 20 seconds.

3. Gradually stir in the flavoured milk. Cook on HIGH for about 3 minutes, stirring frequently, or until the sauce comes to the boil and thickens.

4. Season to taste and, if using, stir in the cream.

To freeze:
Cool and freeze after seasoning in step 4.

Anchovy Sauce

Serve with grilled, steamed or baked fish

Make a White Sauce or Béchamel Sauce. To the hot sauce, add anchovy essence to taste and a good squeeze of fresh lemon juice.

Caper Sauce

Good with fish dishes, lamb and pork.

Make a White Sauce (you may prefer to use half milk and half stock) or Béchamel Sauce. To the hot sauce, stir in 1 tbsp capers (roughly chopped if large) and a dash of wine vinegar or lemon juice.

Cheese Sauce

Serve with vegetables, eggs, bacon, fish or chicken.

Make a White Sauce or Béchamel Sauce. To the hot sauce, add 85-115g/3-4 oz grated mature cheese (Cheddar or Parmesan are good) and ½-1 tsp ready-made mustard (try English, wholegrain or Dijon). Stir until the cheese has melted.

Curry Sauce

Serve with hard-boiled eggs, vegetables, poultry or cold meats.

Make a Traditional White Sauce. Before adding the flour, gently cook some curry paste in the melted butter for about 1 minute. Add a squeeze of fresh lemon juice to the finished sauce.

Egg Sauce

Serve with fish, pasta or vegetables.

Make a White Sauce (using half milk and half fish or vegetable stock) or Béchamel Sauce. To the hot sauce, stir in 1 finely chopped hard-boiled egg and 2 tbsp snipped chives. Reheat gently if necessary.

Not suitable for freezing.

Fresh Herb Sauce

Serve with chicken (use tarragon or chives), fish (try dill or fennel), ham or pork (sage is good), lamb (thyme or oregano) or vegetables (a mixture of fresh herbs is delicious).

Make a White Sauce or Béchamel Sauce. To the hot sauce, stir in 2 tbsp or more of finely chopped fresh herbs.

Garlic Sauce

Serve with vegetables, poultry or meat (lamb in particular).

Make a Traditional White Sauce or Béchamel Sauce. Before adding the flour, gently cook 1-2 crushed garlic cloves in the melted butter until soft but not brown.

Mushroom Sauce

Serve with fish, poultry, meat or pasta.

Make a Traditional White Sauce or Béchamel Sauce. Before adding the flour, fry 85g/3 oz sliced mushrooms in the melted butter until golden brown.

Mustard Sauce

Good with vegetables, beef or ham.

Make a White Sauce or Béchamel Sauce. To the hot sauce, stir in about 2 tbsp ready-made mustard (the wholegrain varieties look pretty and taste good).

Onion Sauce

Serve with roast meats or poultry.

Make a Traditional White Sauce or Béchamel Sauce. Before adding the flour, fry a finely chopped onion in the melted butter until pale golden brown.

Parsley Sauce

Traditionally served with ham, bacon or fish. Good with vegetables and pasta too.

Make a White Sauce or Béchamel Sauce. To the hot sauce, stir in 2 tbsp or more of finely chopped fresh parsley.

Pesto-flavoured Sauce

Try this on vegetables or pasta. Pesto sauce originates from Italy and consists of fresh basil, pine nuts, olive oil and Parmesan cheese. Buy it ready made in jars or make your own (see page 144).

Make a Blended White Sauce. To the hot sauce, stir in 2 tbsp or more of pesto sauce. Reheat gently if necessary.

Prawn Sauce

Serve with fish or pasta.

Make a White Sauce or Béchamel Sauce. To the hot sauce, add 115g/4 oz small peeled prawns and 1 tbsp lemon juice. Heat until bubbling, then serve immediately.

Not suitable for freezing.

Espagnole Sauce

A classic brown sauce which relies on good beef stock (see tip on page 93). It is traditionally served with red meat and game.

Makes about 300ml/½ pt

25g/1 oz butter
1 streaky bacon rasher, rind removed and chopped
1 shallot or very small onion, finely chopped
1 small carrot, finely chopped
2 tbsp flour
425ml/¾ pt good beef stock or consommé
bouquet garni
1 tbsp tomato purée
salt and freshly milled pepper
small knob of butter

1. Melt the butter in a saucepan, add the bacon and cook, stirring occasionally for about 2 minutes. Add the shallot and carrot and cook for about 5 minutes, stirring occasionally, until golden brown. Stir in the flour and cook for 3-4 minutes, stirring frequently, until the mixture is well browned.
2. Remove from the heat and gradually stir in the stock. Cook, stirring, until the sauce comes to the boil and thickens. Add the bouquet garni, tomato purée and seasoning.
3. Simmer very gently for about 1 hour, stirring occasionally to prevent the sauce catching on the bottom of the pan.
4. Strain the sauce and skim off any fat. Adjust the seasoning to taste, add the butter.
5. Reheat before serving.

To freeze:
Cool and freeze at the end of step 4.

TIP:

Instead of using a dried bouquet garni, make a fresh one. Tie together a couple of sprigs each of parsley and thyme, plus one or two fresh bay leaves.

Gravy

A roast dinner would not be the same without gravy. The country seems to be divided between people who prefer their gravy thick and those who prefer it thin.

Makes about 300ml/½ pt

Thin Gravy:
1. Tip the fat from the roasting pan, allowing it to drain away slowly, so that the sediments are left behind. Add about 425ml/¾ pt stock (use cooking water from the vegetables if you have some) or wine or, preferably, a mixture. Season with salt and freshly milled black pepper. Stir well, scraping all the brown sediments from the bottom and sides of the pan.
2. Heat until the mixture comes to the boil, then continue bubbling for about 5 minutes, stirring occasionally, or until slightly reduced.
3. Adjust the seasoning if necessary. If wished, stir in 1-2 tbsp double cream before serving.

Thick Gravy:
1. Pour off the fat from the roasting pan, allowing to drain away slowly, leaving all the sediments and about 1 tbsp fat behind. Stir in 1-2 tbsp flour and cook gently, stirring and scraping all the brown sediments from the bottom and sides of the pan, until it turns brown.
2. Remove from the heat and gradually stir in about 300ml/½ pt stock (use cooking water from the vegetables if you have some) or wine or, preferably, a mixture. Season with salt and freshly milled black pepper.
3. Cook, stirring, until the gravy comes to the boil and thickens. Simmer gently for 2-3 minutes. Adjust the seasoning if necessary.

To freeze:
Cool and freeze at the end of step 3.

TIP:

I like gravy served just as it is, bits of sediment and all, but you may prefer to strain it before serving. A pale gravy can be darkened by adding a little gravy browning, which is flavourless.

Hollandaise Sauce

A classic sauce for serving with, in particular, fish, eggs, asparagus, broccoli or chicken. It is best made just before serving.

Makes about 300ml/½ pt

3 medium egg yolks
1 tbsp white wine vinegar
1 tbsp fresh lemon juice
1 tsp caster sugar
225g/8 oz unsalted butter, softened
salt and freshly milled pepper

1. In a double saucepan or a heatproof bowl standing over a pan of gently simmering water, whisk the egg yolks with the vinegar, lemon juice and sugar until foamy.

2. Making sure the heat beneath is very gentle, continue whisking for 2-3 minutes or until the mixture thickens sufficiently for the whisk to leave a trail on the surface.

3. Remove from the heat and gradually whisk in the butter, one small lump at a time until it has all been incorporated and the sauce has the consistency of mayonnaise. Season to taste with salt and pepper.

TIP:

By cooking very gently, the mixture should not curdle. However, if it does, have an ice cube ready to whisk in – to lower the temperature quickly.

Quick Hollandaise

This recipes uses a food processor to make a sauce which is slightly less creamy, but delicious nonetheless.

Makes about 300ml/¹/₂ pt

3 medium egg yolks
2 tsp white wine vinegar
2 tsp fresh lemon juice
salt and freshly milled pepper
175g/6 oz unsalted butter, softened
1 tsp caster sugar

1. Put the eggs yolks, vinegar, lemon juice and seasoning into a food processor and blend for about 15 seconds until the yolks are creamy.

2. Heat the butter and sugar in a pan until melted and hot, taking care it does not brown.

3. With the food processor running at high speed, gradually add the hot butter in a slow stream until the mixture is thickened, smooth and creamy.

4. Serve immediately.

To microwave:
1. As step 1 above.

2. Put the butter and sugar in a bowl or jug and heat on MEDIUM for about 2 minutes or until melted and hot.

3. Continue with steps 3 and 4 above.

TIP:

Remember, it is not advisable to serve sauces which include eggs which are only lightly cooked to pregnant women or to the very young, elderly or sick.

Mint Sauce

Traditionally served with lamb, this sauce made with fresh mint is much nicer than the bottled variety.

Serves 4-6

about 4 tbsp finely chopped fresh mint leaves
1 tsp caster sugar
2 tbsp white wine or cider vinegar

1. Put the mint and sugar in a bowl and stir in 2 tbsp *boiling* water. Add the vinegar.

2. Leave to stand for at least 1 hour before serving.

To freeze:
Freeze at the end of step 1.

Tartare Sauce

This is a quick version of the sauce which is traditionally served with fish. It's good with egg or vegetable dishes too.

Makes about 300ml/¹/₂ pt

300ml/¹/₂ pt good quality mayonnaise
1 tbsp finely chopped capers
1 tbsp finely chopped fresh parsley or tarragon
2 tbsp finely chopped gherkins

1. Put all the ingredients in a bowl and mix well.

2. Cover and refrigerate for at least 1 hour before serving.

Apple Sauce

A traditional accompaniment to roast or grilled pork, it goes well with duck, goose and game too. I prefer a slightly chunky sauce, but you can sieve or purée it if you like.

Serves 4-6

450g/1 lb cooking apples, peeled, cored and sliced
25g/1 oz caster sugar
1 tbsp lemon juice

1. Put all the ingredients in a saucepan with 1 tbsp water. Cook gently, stirring, until the apples are soft and mushy.

2. Serve warm or at room temperature.

To microwave:
1. Put all the ingredients in a casserole, cover and cook on HIGH for 4-5 minutes, stirring occasionally, or until the apples are soft and mushy.

2. As above.

To freeze:
Cool and freeze at the end of step 1.

Creamy Horseradish Sauce

If you can get fresh horseradish, this is well worth making – so much better than the bottled version. It's traditionally served with beef, mackerel and trout and dishes made with them.

Serves 4

2 tbsp freshly grated horseradish
2 tsp caster sugar
2 tsp white wine vinegar or lemon juice
5 tbsp thick double cream
5 tbsp thick Greek-style yogurt

1. Put the horseradish, sugar and vinegar into a bowl and mix well. Add the cream and yogurt and whisk until light and well blended.

2. Cover and leave to stand, refrigerated, for at least 1 hour before serving cold.

Gooseberry Sauce

Gooseberry sauce should be brought back into fashion! It's delicious served with mackerel, trout and other oily fish. If possible, use freshly grated nutmeg.

Serves 4

350g/12 oz gooseberries, thawed if frozen
25g/1 oz butter
25g/1 oz caster sugar
¼ tsp grated nutmeg
salt and freshly milled pepper

1. Put the gooseberries in a saucepan and add 150ml/¼ pt water. Bring to the boil, then simmer gently for about 5 minutes, stirring occasionally, until soft and tender.

2. Tip into a food processor or liquidiser and purée until smooth. Add the remaining ingredients and purée again for a few seconds.

3. Reheat before serving.

To microwave:
1. Put the gooseberries in a casserole with 125ml/4 fl oz water. Cook on HIGH for about 3 minutes, stirring occasionally, or until the gooseberries are soft and tender.

2. Continue with steps 2 and 3 above.

To freeze:
Cool and freeze at the end of step 2.

Cranberry Sauce

Traditionally, this is served with turkey, though it's good with duck, goose and game too. For a more interesting flavour, use orange juice to cook the cranberries. Alternatively, stir a tablespoon or two of port into the cooked cranberry sauce.

Serves 6

225g/8 oz cranberries
300ml/½ pt water or orange juice
175-225g/6-8 oz sugar

1. Put the cranberries into a saucepan with the water or juice. Cook over medium heat until the mixture comes to the boil, then simmer gently for about 10 minutes or until the cranberries have burst open.

2. Add the sugar and simmer gently, stirring occasionally, until it has dissolved.

3. Serve warm or cold.

To microwave:
1. Put the cranberries into a large casserole with the water or juice. Cook on HIGH for about 3 minutes or until the mixture comes to the boil. Cook on MEDIUM for about 5 minutes or until the cranberries have burst open.

2. Stir in the sugar and cook on MEDIUM for about 5 minutes, stirring occasionally, or until the sugar has dissolved.

3. As step 3 above.

To freeze:
Cool and freeze at the end of step 2.

TIP:

Don't be tempted to add the sugar before the cranberries are tender, otherwise the skins will be tough.

Bread Sauce

A traditional accompaniment to roast poultry. For a velvety finish, add a dash of double cream to the finished sauce.

Serves 4-6

1 small onion, thinly sliced
1 bay leaf
6 black peppercorns
2 cloves
good pinch of grated nutmeg
400ml/14 fl oz milk
55g/2 oz fresh white breadcrumbs
salt and freshly milled pepper
25g/1 oz butter

1. Put the onion into a saucepan with the bay leaf, peppercorns, cloves, nutmeg and milk. Heat slowly until the mixture comes to the boil.

2. Cover and leave to stand for 10-15 minutes, to allow the flavours to infuse into the milk.

3. Strain the milk and return it to the pan. Stir in the breadcrumbs and seasoning.

4. Cover and simmer very gently for about 10 minutes, stirring occasionally.

5. Stir in the butter.

To microwave:
1. Put the onion into a casserole with the bay leaf, peppercorns, cloves, nutmeg and milk. Cook uncovered on HIGH for about 3 minutes or until the mixture comes to the boil.

2. As step 2 above.

3. As step 3 above.

4. Cover and cook on MEDIUM for about 5 minutes, stirring occasionally, or until the sauce is thick and creamy.

5. As step 5 above.

To freeze:
Cool and freeze at the end of step 5.

Tomato Sauce

Good served with pasta, vegetables, fish, meat or poultry. I like to serve the sauce as it is, but if you prefer a smooth version, then either pass it through a nylon sieve or purée it in the food processor or liquidiser.

Serves 4-6

1 tbsp olive oil
1 small onion, finely chopped
1 small carrot, finely chopped
1 small celery stick, finely chopped
1 plump garlic clove, finely chopped or crushed
400g can chopped tomatoes or 450g/1 lb fresh ripe tomatoes, skinned and chopped
300ml/½ pt chicken or vegetable stock
1 tbsp tomato purée
1 tbsp sugar
1 tbsp chopped fresh herbs, such as thyme, basil or parsley
salt and freshly milled pepper

1. Heat the oil in a pan and cook the onion, carrot, celery and garlic for about 5 minutes, stirring occasionally, until soft but not brown.

2. Stir in the remaining ingredients. Bring to the boil, cover and simmer gently for about 15 minutes or until the vegetables are very tender.

3. If you want a thicker sauce, continue cooking, uncovered, for 3-5 minutes until the sauce has reduced slightly.

To microwave:
1. Put the oil into a large casserole and stir in the onion, carrot, celery and garlic. Cover and cook on HIGH for about 3 minutes or until soft.

2. Stir in the remaining ingredients. Cover and cook on HIGH for about 10 minutes, stirring occasionally.

3. If you want a thicker sauce, continue cooking, uncovered, on MEDIUM for about 5 minutes, or until the sauce has reduced slightly.

To freeze:
Cool and freeze at the end of step 3.

Barbecue Sauce

This sauce is great served with grilled or barbecued meats such as chops, chicken, sausages and burgers. It can be used as a glaze too – brush it over the food half way through cooking. If you want to try something a little different, use stout in place of the water in step 2.

Serves 4-6

1 tbsp oil
1 medium onion, finely chopped
2 plump garlic cloves, finely chopped or crushed
3 tbsp tomato ketchup
2 tbsp tomato purée
2 tbsp Worcestershire sauce
1 tbsp malt vinegar
1 tbsp soft brown sugar
1 tbsp ready-made mustard, such as Dijon
salt and freshly milled pepper

1. Heat the oil in a pan and add the onion and garlic. Cook for about 5 minutes, stirring occasionally, until soft but not brown.

2. Add 150ml/¼ pt water *(see note above)* and stir in the remaining ingredients.

3. Bring to the boil, cover and simmer gently for 15-20 minutes, stirring occasionally.

4. If you prefer a thicker consistency, remove the cover and simmer gently for a further 5-10 minutes until the sauce has reduced.

To microwave:
1. Put the oil, onion and garlic in a casserole, cover and cook on HIGH for 3 minutes or until soft.

2. As step 2 above.

3. Cover and cook on MED-HIGH for 8-10 minutes, stirring occasionally.

4. If you prefer a thicker consistency, cook uncovered on MED-HIGH for 3-5 minutes until the sauce has reduced.

To freeze:
Cool and freeze at the end of step 4.

Sweet and Sour Sauce

A deliciously fruity and chunky sauce, ideal for serving with grilled or barbecued meats, poultry, fish or vegetables.

Serves 6

1 tbsp oil
1 medium onion, thinly sliced
1 plump garlic clove, finely chopped or crushed
1 small green pepper, seeds removed and sliced
400g can chopped tomatoes
4 tbsp soft brown sugar
1 tsp mixed dried herbs
220g can pineapple chunks in fruit juice
1 tbsp cornflour
2 tbsp wine vinegar
2 tbsp light soy sauce
salt and freshly milled pepper

1. Heat the oil in a pan and add the onion, garlic and green pepper. Cook gently for about 5 minutes, stirring occasionally, until soft but not brown.

2. Stir in the tomatoes, sugar, herbs and 85ml/3 fl oz water. Drain the pineapple, adding the juice to the pan. Blend the cornflour with the vinegar and soy sauce and stir into the pan.

3. Bring to the boil, stirring continuously, until the sauce comes to the boil and thickens. Simmer gently for about 5 minutes,

4. Season to taste and stir in the pineapple chunks. Heat through before serving.

To microwave:

1. Put the oil into a casserole and stir in the onion, garlic and green pepper. Cover and cook on HIGH for about 5 minutes, stirring once, until soft.

2. As step 2 above.

3. Cook on HIGH for about 5 minutes, stirring occasionally, or until the sauce comes to the boil and thickens. Cook on MEDIUM for 3 minutes.

4. Continue as step 4 above.

To freeze:
Cool and freeze at the end of step 4.

Peanut Satay Sauce

The quantity of sauce may seem small for four servings, but it is quite rich. I like to use crunchy peanut butter, but use the smooth variety if you prefer. Serve with chicken or lamb kebabs or grilled chops and burgers.

Serves 4

1 tbsp oil
1 medium onion, finely chopped
1 plump garlic clove, finely chopped or crushed
3 tbsp soy sauce
finely grated rind and juice of 1 lemon
1 tbsp sweet chilli sauce
4 tbsp peanut butter
1 tbsp dark brown sugar
125ml/4 fl oz vegetable stock
salt and freshly milled pepper

1. Heat the oil in a pan and add the onion and garlic. Cook gently for about 5 minutes, stirring frequently, until soft but not brown.

2. Stir in the remaining ingredients and cook gently, stirring, until the mixture comes to the boil.

To microwave:
1. Put the oil, onion and garlic in a casserole and cook on HIGH for 2 minutes or until soft.

2. Stir in the remaining ingredients and cook on HIGH for about 3 minutes, stirring frequently, until the sauce comes to the boil.

Not suitable for freezing.

Creamy Fish Sauce

If you have some, home-made fish stock is wonderful in this sauce.
Serve it with poached or steamed fish.

Makes just over 300ml/½ pt

300ml/½ pt fish stock
150ml/¼ pt white wine or dry vermouth
150ml/¼ pt double cream
1 tbsp chopped fresh herbs, such as dill, fennel or parsley
salt and freshly milled pepper

1. Put the stock and wine into a saucepan and bring to the boil.
   Simmer gently until the mixture has reduced by about half.

2. Stir in the cream and herbs. Season to taste with salt and pepper.
   Heat gently until bubbling.

To microwave:
1. Put the stock and wine into a casserole and cook, uncovered, on
   HIGH for about 3 minutes or until the mixture comes to the boil.
   Continue cooking on HIGH, checking frequently, until the mixture
   has reduced by about half.

2. Stir in the cream and herbs, Season to taste with salt and pepper.
   Cook on HIGH for about 1 minute or until bubbling.

Not suitable for freezing.

Pesto Sauce

Based on the traditional Italian sauce for stirring into hot pasta. It can be bought in jars, but home made is so much better. If you don't have enough basil, use some parsley as well.

Makes about 300ml/¹/₂ pt

55g/2 oz piece of fresh Parmesan or Pecorino cheese
25g/1 oz pine kernels, toasted
55g/2 oz fresh basil leaves
2 plump garlic cloves
good pinch of salt
175ml/6 fl oz olive oil

1. Remove any rind from the cheese and cut into small cubes. Put into a food processor and blend until the mixture looks like fine breadcrumbs.

2. Add the pine kernels and buzz again.

3. Add the basil, garlic and salt and buzz again.

4. With the processor running, pour in the oil in a steady stream.

5. Spoon into a jar and store in the refrigerator.

To freeze:
At the end of step 4.

Bolognese Sauce

This is my family's favourite recipe for meat sauce. Serve it on freshly cooked spaghetti or as a filling for jacket potatoes.

Serves 4

1 tbsp oil
1 large onion, finely chopped
1 plump garlic clove, finely chopped or crushed
4 lean streaky bacon rashers, rinds removed and finely chopped
2 medium carrots, finely chopped
450g/1 lb lean minced beef
150ml/¼ pt beef stock or consommé (see tip on page 93), plus extra if necessary
2 tbsp tomato purée
1 tsp dried herbs, such as oregano and thyme
salt and freshly milled pepper

1. Heat the oil in a pan and add the onion, garlic, bacon and carrots. Cook gently for 5-10 minutes, stirring occasionally, until soft and just beginning to brown.

2. Add the minced beef, stirring to break it up, and cook for 5 minutes until it is brown.

3. Add the remaining ingredients and bring to the boil. Cover and simmer gently for about 45 minutes, adding extra stock if the mixture becomes too dry.

To microwave:
1. Put the oil into a large casserole and stir in the onion, garlic, bacon and carrots. Cover and cook on HIGH for about 5 minutes, stirring once, until soft.

2. Add the minced beef, breaking it up with a fork. Cover and cook on HIGH for about 5 minutes, stirring once or twice.

3. Stir in the remaining ingredients. Cover and cook on HIGH for 10 minutes, then on MEDIUM for 5-10 minutes, stirring once or twice, until the beef is very tender.

To freeze:
Cool and freeze at the end of step 3.

10

QUICK SAUCES TO SERVE
WITH PASTA OR RICE

These recipes were originally created for the microwave with my
friend and colleague, Caroline Young. They have adapted perfectly
well to cooking on the hob and are meant to be tossed with hot pasta
or served on freshly-cooked rice. The first two recipes need no
cooking at all. Quantities are sufficient for two servings (for four,
simply double the amounts and cook for a little longer).

Sun-Dried Tomato and Olive Sauce

6 sun-dried tomatoes in oil, drained
55g/2 oz pitted black olives, chopped
1 tbsp chopped fresh thyme leaves
salt and freshly milled pepper

1. Mix the ingredients with 3 tbsp oil from the tomatoes and stir straight into hot pasta or rice.

Anchovy and Parsley Sauce

50g can anchovies
3 tbsp chopped fresh parsley
freshly milled black pepper

1. Drain the anchovies, reserving the oil. Finely chop the anchovies and mix them with the parsley. Stir in the oil. Toss the mixture straight into hot pasta or rice.

Mushrooms and Herb Cheese Sauce

115g/4 oz button mushrooms, sliced
150ml/¼ pt vegetable stock
50g packet soft cheese with herbs and garlic
salt and freshly milled pepper

1. Put the mushrooms and stock into a small pan, cover and bring to the boil. Simmer gently for 1-2 minutes until soft.

2. Gradually stir in the cheese and heat gently until melted. Season to taste.

To microwave:
1. Put the mushrooms and stock into a bowl, cover and cook on HIGH for 2-3 minutes until soft.

2. Gradually stir in the cheese and cook on MEDIUM for about 2 minutes or until melted. Season to taste.

Tuna and Tomato Sauce

2 tsp oil
1 small onion, finely chopped
1 plump garlic clove, finely chopped or crushed
230g can chopped tomatoes
1 tsp wine vinegar
salt and freshly milled pepper
200g can tuna in brine, drained and flaked

1. Put the oil in a small pan and add the onion and garlic, Cook gently for about 5 minutes until very soft but not brown.

2. Add the remaining ingredients and heat gently, stirring occasionally, until bubbling hot.

To microwave:
1. Put the oil, onion and garlic into a bowl and cook on HIGH for 1-2 minutes until very soft.

2. Stir in the remaining ingredients and cook on MEDIUM, stirring occasionally, until bubbling hot.

Green Onion and Herb Sauce

55g/2 oz butter
4 spring onions, thinly sliced
1 plump garlic clove, crushed
2 tbsp chopped fresh parsley
2 tbsp snipped chives

1. Melt the butter in a small pan and add the onions and garlic. Cook very gently for 1-2 minutes until the onions are just soft. Stir in the herbs.

To microwave:
1. Put the butter, onions and garlic into a small bowl. Cook on HIGH for about 1 minute until bubbling hot. Stir in the herbs.

Mushrooms and Soured Cream Sauce

25g/1 oz butter
115g/4 oz button or cup mushrooms, thinly sliced
150ml/¼ pt soured cream
salt and freshly milled pepper
1 tbsp chopped fresh parsley

1. Melt the butter in a small pan and add the mushrooms. Cook gently, stirring occasionally, until golden brown.

2. Stir in the cream and heat gently until bubbling hot. Season to taste and stir in the parsley.

To microwave:
1. Put the butter and mushrooms into a bowl and cook on HIGH for about 2 minutes, stirring once, until just soft.

2. Stir in the cream and heat on HIGH for about 1 minute until bubbling hot. Season to taste and stir in the parsley.

Curried Prawn Sauce

2 tsp cornflour
150ml/¼ pt milk
15g/½ oz butter
2 tsp curry paste
salt and freshly milled pepper
115g/4 oz small cooked and peeled prawns (fresh, canned or thawed if frozen)

1. In a small pan, blend the cornflour with the milk, then add the butter. Heat gently, whisking continuously, until the sauce comes to the boil and thickens.

2. Whisk in the curry paste and season to taste. Stir in the prawns and heat gently until bubbling hot.

To microwave:
1. In a bowl, blend the cornflour with the milk, then add the butter. Cook on HIGH for 1-2 minutes, whisking once or twice, until the sauce comes to the boil and thickens.

2. Whisk in the curry paste and season to taste. Stir in the prawns and cook on HIGH for about 45 seconds until bubbling hot.

11

SWEET SAUCES

Sweet White Sauce

Traditionally served with sponge puddings. This is the plain version, but do try it flavoured with almond essence, extra vanilla extract (to make Vanilla Sauce) or some finely grated lemon or orange rind.

Makes about 300ml/½ pt

1 tbsp cornflour
300ml/½ pt milk
1 tbsp caster sugar
few drops of vanilla extract
knob of butter (optional)

1. Put the cornflour in a bowl and blend it with a little of the milk to make a smooth paste. Put the remaining milk and the sugar into a saucepan and bring just to the boil. Pour on to the cornflour mixture, stirring continuously.
2. Return the mixture to the pan and cook, stirring, until the sauce comes to the boil and thickens.
3. Cook very gently for 2-3 minutes, stirring. Add the vanilla and the butter, if using.

To microwave:
1. Put the cornflour in a bowl or jug and blend with a little of the milk to make a smooth paste. Stir in the remaining milk and add the sugar.
2. Cook on MEDIUM for about 3 minutes, whisking frequently, or until the sauce comes to the boil, thickens and is cooked.
3. Add the vanilla and the butter, if using.

To freeze:
Cool and freeze at the end of step 3.

Brandy Sauce and Rum Sauce

Especially good with Christmas pudding.

Make the Sweet White Sauce, omitting the vanilla extract and adding 2 tbsp brandy or rum in step 3.

Chocolate Sauce

Serve with chocolate sponge pudding or poached pears.

Make the Sweet White Sauce, stirring 1 tbsp cocoa powder into the cornflour in step 1. If you like, add 25-55g/1-2 oz grated plain chocolate too.

Custard Sauce

For occasions when custard powder or packets of ready made custard are just not good enough, this is sheer luxury. Serve, hot or cold, with all kinds of fruit, puddings, pies.

Makes 600ml/1 pt

1 vanilla pod
300ml/½ pt milk
300ml/½ pt single cream
4 medium egg yolks
55g/2 oz caster sugar

1. Split the vanilla pod and put the seeds and pod into a saucepan. Add the milk and cream. Heat gently until the mixture just comes to the boil. Remove from the heat and leave to stand for 15-20 minutes while the flavour infuses into the milk.
2. In a large bowl, beat the egg yolks with the sugar until well blended.
3. Reheat the milk and cream mixture until very hot and bubbles form on the surface (but do not allow it to boil). From a height, gradually pour the mixture on to the yolks, beating well.
4. Strain through a fine sieve and return the mixture to the pan.
5. Making sure the heat beneath is very, very gentle, cook, stirring continuously, until the custard thickens to the consistency of single cream (it should leave a thin coating on the back of the spoon). Take care not to heat it too much or the mixture will curdle.

To microwave:
Use your microwave to heat the milk in steps 1 and 3. Though I prefer to complete step 5 on the hob, it is possible to thicken the custard in the microwave. Use a substantial heatproof bowl and cook on MED-LOW, stirring very frequently and taking care not to allow the custard to overheat and curdle.

TIP:

To prevent the custard from curdling, add 1 tsp cornflour in step 2.

If you want the custard to thicken on cooling, for a trifle perhaps, stir 2 tsp cornflour into the egg yolks in step 2.

See also page 132.

Real Chocolate Sauce

Spoon over ice cream, profiteroles and desserts containing pears. For the best flavour, use a plain chocolate with 50% or more cocoa solids.

Serves 4-6

175g/6 oz plain chocolate
3 tbsp golden syrup
1 tbsp fresh lemon or orange juice
knob of butter

1. Break the chocolate into a small pan and add the syrup, juice, butter and 2 tbsp water.

2. Heat very gently, stirring occasionally, until the chocolate has melted and is smooth and glossy.

To microwave:
1. Break the chocolate into a bowl and add the syrup, juice, butter and 2 tbsp water.

2. Cook on MEDIUM for 2-3 minutes, stirring frequently, until the chocolate has melted and is smooth and glossy.

Not suitable for freezing.

Butterscotch Sauce

Particularly delicious with ice cream and desserts containing bananas or chocolate.

Serves 4-6

55g/2 oz butter
55g/2 oz soft brown sugar
175g/6 oz golden syrup
2 tsp lemon juice
150ml/¼ pt double cream

1. Put the butter, sugar and syrup into a small pan and heat gently, stirring occasionally, until the butter has melted. Stir until well blended.

2. Stir in the lemon juice and cream and heat gently until bubbling.

To microwave:
1. Put the butter, sugar and syrup into a bowl or jug. Cook on HIGH for about 2 minutes, stirring once or twice, until the butter has melted. Stir until well blended.

2. Stir in the lemon juice and cream and cook on HIGH for ½-1 minute or until just bubbling.

To freeze:
Cool and freeze at the end of step 2.

Jam Sauce and Marmalade Sauce

A really quick sauce to serve with sponge puddings or poached fruit.

Serves 4-6

2 tsp cornflour
4 tbsp jam or marmalade
1 tsp lemon juice

1. Measure 150ml/¼ pt cold water. Blend the cornflour with a little of the water to make a smooth paste.

2. Pour the remaining water into a small pan and add the jam or marmalade and lemon juice. Heat gently until the jam has just melted.

3. Remove the pan from the heat and stir in the cornflour mixture.

4. Cook, stirring continuously, until the sauce comes to the boil and thickens.

To microwave:
1. As step 1 above.

2. Pour the remaining water into a bowl and add the jam or marmalade and lemon juice. Heat on HIGH for about 1½ minutes, stirring once, or until the jam has melted.

3. Stir in the cornflour mixture, then cook on MEDIUM for about 2 minutes, stirring once or twice, until the sauce comes to the boil and thickens.

Not suitable for freezing.

Summer Berry Fruit Sauce

Fresh tasting and simple to make. Serve as a topping for ice cream or to accompany slices of gateaux or cheesecake. Use one type of berry (raspberries are excellent) or a mixture (choose from raspberries, blackberries, strawberries, blackcurrants, redcurrants, blueberries).

Makes about 300ml/½ pt

250g/9 oz summer berries, thawed if frozen
2 tsp lemon juice
icing sugar
2 tbsp fruit liqueur, such as Cointreau (orange), framboise (raspberry) or cassis (blackcurrant)

1. Tip the fruit into a food processor or liquidiser and add the lemon juice and 2 tbsp sugar. Purée until smooth. Adjust the sweetness, adding sugar according to taste and what you will be serving with the sauce (a very sweet dessert will be nicer with a sharper sauce, for instance).

2. Pass the sauce through a fine nylon sieve to remove the seeds.

3. Stir in the liqueur.

To freeze:
Freeze at the end of step 2. Add the liqueur once the sauce has thawed.

INDEX